The Witches' Almanac

Spring 2008 — Spring 2009

CONTAINING pictorial and explicit delineations of the
magical phases of the Moon together with information about astrological
portents of the year to come and various aspects of occult knowledge
enabling all who read to improve their lives in the old manner.

The Witches' Almanac, Ltd.

Publishers   Newport, Rhode Island
www.TheWitchesAlmanac.com

Address all inquiries and information to
THE WITCHES' ALMANAC, LTD.
P.O. Box 1292
Newport, RI 02840-9998

10-ISBN: 0-9773703-3-X
13-ISBN: 978-0-9773703-3-7

ISSN: 1522-3183

First Printing September 2007

Printed in the United States of America

Established 1971 by Elizabeth Pepper

Preface

This year we dedicate *The Witches' Almanac* to the art of divination and prophecy. Mankind has always had a fascination with the indeterminable future. We fear the negative experiences that we may encounter, yet we still desire to know our future. We are aided by gifted people with the ability to see into another's future. Every psychic has experienced their gift as both a blessing and a curse. Seeing another's future carries with it a heavy burden.

Most people seeking unforeseen knowledge assume that what a seer tells them is the future apparent. This is not always the case. The gift to see the future gives a glimpse of myriad possibilities. Some indications may be true, while others are only a "wish list" or "fear list" of possibilities.

A diviner will report the tendencies of the future given the current situation, yet each of us holds the power to change that future. Before coming into this life, we chose our path and life's goal. Still, our chosen destination remains in check and balance with our free will. Given the choice, would you glance into your future?

This issue of *The Witches' Almanac* presents insight into the quest for knowledge through the time-honored tradition of prophecy. Remember, the only one who can create your future is you. You do it all the time!

Almanac Extras

With each Almanac, we have more related material than space. A delightful problem. So we have added "Almanac Extras" on our website – supplements to text in print. We will also occasionally offer a "Bonus Feature," an entire web article related to a topic in a current issue. This year our website has additional material on Dr. Emoto and his water experiments, Yoruba practices of divination, tea-leaf formations, and more. Of course, we will continue with our delectable monthly recipe and weekly spell from the *Encyclopedia of 5,000 Spells*. Further explore at *www.TheWitchesAlmanac.com*.

HOLIDAYS

Spring 2008 to Spring 2009

✳

Astrologer   Dikki-Jo Mullen
Climatologist   Tom C. Lang
Production Consultant   Robin Antoni
Art Director   Karen Marks
Sales   Ellen Lynch
Shipping, Bookkeeping   Doreen Bullock

CONTENTS

✳

ANDREW THEITIC – Executive Editor

BARBARA STACY, JEAN MARIE WALSH
Associate Editors

Jonathan Swift Somers

After you have enriched your soul
To the highest point,
With books, thought, suffering, the understanding
of many personalities,
The power to interpret glances, silences,
The pauses in momentous transformations,
The genius of divination and prophecy;
So that you feel able at times to hold the world
In the hollow of your hand;
Then, if, by the crowding of so many powers
Into the compass of your soul,
Your soul takes fire,
And in the conflagration of your soul
The evil of the world is lighted up and made clear —
Be thankful if in that hour of supreme vision
Life does not fiddle.

– *Spoon River Anthology*
EDGAR LEE MASTERS, 1916

H. Nisle

Yesterday, Today and Tomorrow

by Herb McSidhe

DEATH BY FAIRIES. A document listing deaths from 1656 to 1663 in the parish of Lamplugh, Cumbria, was found in archives as part of a national campaign to uncover treasures of local history. The single sheet of paper from a parish burial register paints a gripping and sometimes comical picture of England in the mid-seventeenth century. Four people were "Frighted to Death by fairies," according to the verbatim report. Another perished after he was "Led into a horse pond by a will of the wisp." Cumbria county archivist Anne Rowe said: "I've never come across anything like it before. Many people have been terrified of fairies, but I'm not sure whether this list reflects ancestral superstitions or sense of humour."

NOT MY GRANNIE! The grand-daughter of the "last person in Britain to be tried as a witch" has vowed she and her family would never give up the fight to clear her relative's name. Helen Duncan, of Niddrie, Edinburgh, traveled the country performing seances at which she claimed to contact people killed during World War II. In 1944, she was convicted under the 1735 Witchcraft Act of "pretending to raise the spirits of the dead" and sentenced to nine months in jail. Her granddaughter, Mary Martin, applied in 1999 to Jack Straw, then home secretary, for a posthumous pardon. Straw refused. Legend notwithstanding, Duncan was not the "last person to be prosecuted under the Witchcraft Act." It was invoked as late as December 1944, when police warned Emily Johnson of the Redhill Spiritualist Church that if her activities continued she would be liable to prosecution. The charge must have stopped – or slowed down – her "activities," as no trial record exists.

AZTEC RAINMAKERS. Scuba divers in a frigid volcanic lake near Mexico City came up with more than shivers – scepters topped with the jagged forms of lightning bolts. The wooden artifacts also included cones of copal incense and obsidian knives more than five hundred years old. Priestly journals of the Spanish conquest reveal that the Aztecs made offerings to a rain god. Long sticks topped with lightning shapes "were used by Aztec priests when they were doing rites associated with the god Tlaloc," states anthropologist

Johan Reinhard, a diver at the Lake of the Moon. Experts believe that the scepters were left in the lake to bring rain storms and incense was burned to encourage clouds. The sharp objects, knives and cactus spines, indicated that worshippers drew blood from themselves as part of the sacrifice. But archaeologist Luis Alberto Martos differs. He asserts that the ritual may date way back to 100 B.C., long before the Aztecs settled the region in 1325.

BEE GONE! The absence of honeybees has added to America's environmental nightmares, an event so serious as to require a name. Beekeepers in 24 states report record losses of honeybees, now termed "beehive colony collapse disorder," and some areas report a 70 percent drop in bee populations. "I have never seen anything like it," said California beekeeper David Bradshaw. "Box after box after box is just empty. There's nobody home."

Why is the phenomenon so drastic? A Cornell University study estimated that honeybees annually pollinate more than 14 billion dollars worth of seeds and crops in the United States, mostly fruits, vegetables and nuts. "Every third bite we consume in our diet is dependent on a honeybee to pollinate that food," said Zac Browning, vice-president of the American Beekeeping Federation. The U.S. bee population had already been shocked in recent years by a tiny parasitic bug, the varroa mite, which has destroyed more than half of some beekeepers' hives and devastated most wild honeybee populations.

An analysis of dissected bees turned up an alarmingly high number of foreign fungi, bacteria, other organisms and weakened immune systems. Researchers are also looking into the effect genetically engineered pollen or pesticide toxicity might be having on bees. Another area of concern is the possibility that the increased use of wireless telephone signals might be disrupting the bees' innate navigation ability to find their own hives.

NUTTER BLOOD. A hundred-year-old Englishwoman celebrating her landmark birthday last year said her long life could be linked to a distant relation. Una Gartside attributes her longevity to witch's blood. According to 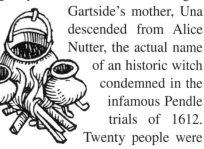 Gartside's mother, Una descended from Alice Nutter, the actual name of an historic witch condemned in the infamous Pendle trials of 1612. Twenty people were

tried, ranging in age from nine to eighty years old and condemned on evidence stemming from idle gossip, false accusations, and rumors. But Gartside believes she benefits from the Nutter bloodline. "I think I must have some kind of power passed on, because I've been very lucky. I've got very good instincts – if that little voice in my head tells me to do something or take a particular choice, I always end up sorry if I don't." But Gartside adds, "I haven't been so lucky with the bingo, though. I haven't won anything for a year."

ZEUS AND HERA, TOGETHER AGAIN. Current recognition by the Greek government of Ellinais, a modern pagan group, has inspired members to honor Zeus at a 1,800-year-old temple in the heart of Athens. The ritual was the first ceremony of its kind on the site since the ancient Greek religion was outlawed in the fourth century, when Emperor Constantine converted to Christianity. The group celebrated despite a ban by the Culture Ministry, which declared the temple off limits to everyone in order to protect the monument. Worshippers assembled at the shrine's imposing Corinthian columns and made no attempt to enter the temple. No officials sought to stop the ceremony, celebrating the nuptials of Zeus and Hera, the goddess of love and marriage, the Queen of Olympus especially adored by women. Dressed in ancient costumes, pagans recited hymns calling on the Olympian Zeus, "King of the gods and the mover of things," to bring peace to the world. "Our message is world peace and an ecological way of life in which everyone has the right to education," said Kostas Stathopoulos, one of three "high priests" overseeing the event.

DURRINGTON WALLS, DIG UP-DATE. The ancient settlement, two miles north of Stonehenge, continues to yield intriguing clues for archaeologists. The huge dig, begun in 2004, apparently served as home for the builders of Stonehenge. The Neolithic community dates from around 2600 BC, the same period the iconic blocks were erected at Stonehenge. As for any "henge," it is a circular structure, this one about a mile in diameter. Within were houses for hundreds of workers and such huge middens of bones and artifacts as to

suggest a site of ritual feasting. But archaeologists have now discovered two houses on a higher terrace overlooking the main settlement, suggesting that they are significant structures. Unlike other buildings, the remains of these two sites were surrounded by timber palisades and free of debris. The houses may have belonged to community leaders or priests, or they may have served as shrines.

PROTECT MUMMY FROM SNAKES. The sophisticated ancient Egyptians considered themselves superior to their contemporaries, but sometimes they called on outsiders for help in magic. A spell to discourage snakes from the tombs of Egyptian kings was adapted from Semitic Canaanites almost five thousand years ago, and could be the oldest existing Semitic text. The phrases, interspersed throughout Egyptian characters in the underground chambers of a pyramid south of Cairo, stumped experts for about a century. Then the mysterious inscriptions came to the attention of Richard Steiner, a professor of Semitic languages at Yeshiva University in New York. Steiner discovered that the symbols were Proto-Canaanite, the direct ancestor of biblical Hebrew used sometime between 30 to 25 B.C. "I immediately recognized the words

'mother snake,'" Steiner told the *National Geographic News*. "It was hiding there in plain sight." Obviously an aha experience! It's unintelligible to Egyptologists, but it makes perfect sense to Semitists. According to Steiner, the Egyptians consulted Canaanite priests because some of the poisonous snakes so feared in Egypt were thought to understand Canaanite. "You need somebody with good connections to the snake. You can't just come along and say, get out of here, snake. Why should the snake listen to you? You need to involve someone who commands the snake's respect, someone who can speak to the snake in its own language and who is related to it in some way, its mother or lover. That's the whole nature of Egyptian magic. In order to counter the bad guys, you need to enlist somebody close to them." According to the incantation, female snakes – acting as mediators for Canaanite magicians – used their multiple mouths and sexual organs to prevent other snakes from entering the mummified ruler's remains. Not a pretty thought. But the linguistic breakthrough from Steiner's discovery is beautiful. The newly deciphered spells may provide scholars with the first glimpse of the ancestor language to Phoenician and Hebrew.

The Sphere of the Fixed Stars, from a 15th-century Italian tarocchi *deck.*

DIVINATION, as any witch worth his or her salt can tell you, may be defined as the attempt to elicit information from some occult entity or some deeply hidden dimension of the mind, information often considered beyond the reach of our rationality. Such questions are usually about future events, inexplicable past disasters, things hidden from sight or distant in space, and so on. As a practice, divination has its roots in very ancient history, in Babylon and Egypt and China.

In the past almost anything could be, and was, used to divine by: the entrails of sacrificial animals, the features of the human body, the stars, the weather, the elements, flights of birds. Sometimes the will of fate or the goddess Fortune, as the Romans named her, was discerned by casting or drawing lots, symbols or runes or alphabetical letters inscribed on bones, dice or slips of wood. Each divination system worked differently, but basically each symbol was associated by tradition with a certain meaning when it showed up. This type of divination carried the Old French term *sortilege*, derived from the Latin *sortilegium*. In medieval Europe bibliomancy, a type of sortilege available to the literate man or woman, became popular. You obtained guidance by randomly opening what you considered a book dealing with the activity of divine powers, a copy of the Bible, the *Iliad* or the *Aeneid*, perhaps, and with eyes closed, pricking a line of text with a needle and interpreting it as an oracle. One of the fathers of the Christian church, Saint Augustine himself, confessed to using this type of sortilege in times of crisis.

The Minor Arcana, the Major Arcana
By the fifteenth century Italian playing cards known as *tarocchi* or Tarots were also being used for sortilege, the individual cards being used to prompt

the intuitions of the diviner. Tarot cards and what we think of today as regular playing cards are not quite the same thing, although they are close cousins. The Tarot deck appeared out of the blue during the fifteenth century as a colorful variant of the standard northern-Italian playing card deck in either Milan, Ferrara, or Bologna – Tarot historians haven't quite made up their minds about the town yet.

One of the earliest Tarot decks, the Milanese, was probably introduced to France by French soldiers returning from their occupation of Milan between 1495 and 1525. The French so-called "Marseilles" pattern appears to have been copied from these Milanese cards, and represents what most people today regard as the conventional Tarot deck. The 56 cards in 4 suits, which actually constitute the cards of the traditional standard Italian playing card deck, make up what witches have come to know today as the *Minor Arcana:* Coins (sometimes referred to as Pentacles), Cups, Swords, and Batons (sometimes referred to as Wands). Each suit contains 14 cards: 10 numeral "pip" cards and 4 colorful "Court" cards, a Knave or Page, Knight, Queen, and King.

To these have been added – and this is what makes the Tarot special – 22 mysterious picture cards generally known as Trumps, but to witches as the *Major Arcana.* In

the old Italian game of Tarot, a Trump card can beat any suit card that is played and win the trick. The Trumps depict a variety of evocative medieval images: a Fool, a Juggler, a Female Pope, an Empress, an Emperor, a

Male Pope, a pair of Lovers, a Chariot, the Virtue of Justice, a Hermit, the Wheel of the goddess Fortune, the Virtue of Fortitude, a Man hanging upside down, usually by one foot, the figure of Death, the Virtue Temperance, the Devil, a lightning-struck Tower, a Star, the Moon, the Sun, a figure of the World, and finally the Last Judgment. The inclusion of the Female Pope – in all probability a depiction of the mythical ninth-century nun named Joan who, on account of her wisdom, was allegedly elected pope as John VIII – indicates that, when considered as a unit or set, the Trump sequence may well be a sort of compendium of the medieval drama, where Joan was the frequent subject of German miracle plays. The other figures and devices in the Trump parade serve to confirm this notion, for they all appear in the imagery of mystery, miracle, or morality plays of the era, many in fact, in the morality play known as *The Dance of Death.* The Trumps of the Tarot deck basically seem to tell the story of the soul's journey through life into the afterlife, an archetypal and perennial story encountered in mythology the world over, but here recounted in the imagery of late medieval Christendom.

Cartomancy, a more complex reading

However, although it was practiced from the fifteenth century onward, the art of playing card sortilege appears to have remained a relatively simple pastime, more for entertainment than anything else, until the invention of "cartomancy," a more complex method of reading cards in rows and matrices, which only evolved in the eighteenth century. The man responsible, a Parisian diviner named Jean-Baptiste Alliette, claimed he had been instructed in an elementary version of the art by three traditional card readers, one of whom was from Piedmont, Italy. Etteilla appears to have drawn his interpretations of the suit cards from the traditional lore of these instructors. For his interpretations of the 22 Trumps, however, he drew on the researches of two occultist Freemasons, Antoine Court de Gébelin and Louis de Fayolle, Comte de Mellet, who were confident that the Tarot originated in Ancient Egypt, a notion that Etteilla also adopted.

Etteilla's ideas, as set down by his pupils, laid the groundwork for what one might call today's Tarot mystique. Inevitably he had a host of imitators, but it required the ingenuity of Alphonse Louis Constant, a Roman Catholic ex-deacon who turned occultist and wrote under the pen name of Éliphas Lévi, and who actually despised the ideas of Etteilla, to expand upon the theory initially advanced by De Gébelin and De Mellet that the 22 Trumps were linked, in a cabalistic manner, to the 22 letters of the Hebrew alphabet. In doing this, Lévi was actually blending ideas proposed by De Gébelin with the ruminations of a seventeenth-century philologist, Athanasius Kircher, who in his work *Oedipus Aegyptiacus* had presented a table of the 22 Hebrew letters alongside what he considered to be their true meanings (nothing like their real Hebrew translations, alas), and equated it with the entire cosmos of the Renaissance, a world consisting of angels, heavens, fixed stars, planets and the four elements.

For good measure, Levi also equated the four suits with the four letters composing the principal Hebrew name of God, JHVH, which he also linked with the four elements, Fire, Air, Earth and Water.

While Etteilla's ideas became the driving force in Europe behind Tarot divination, in England and America Lévi's cabalistic system became preeminent. It found its way into the light of day via the work of two of the founders of an English Rosicrucian society known as the Hermetic Order of the Golden Dawn. In or around 1888, Wynn Westcott and Samuel MacGregor Mathers adopted Lévi's Tarot scheme into the teachings of their Order, but augmented Etteilla's interpretations of the suit cards, which Lévi had left basically untouched, by matching the 36 Twos through Tens with the interpretations of the 36 zodiacal decans to be found in an influential thirteenth-century grimoire of Arabic astrological magic known as *The Picatrix*.

Waite's divinatory visions

None of these complexities were apparent, however, when in 1910 Arthur Edward Waite, a prolific author on mystical subjects and a sometime member of Mathers's Order, introduced the British and American public to the Tarot in his book *The Pictorial Key to the Tarot*. This book (and subsequently a deck of cards) supplied illustrations of the divinatory meanings for every card, not just the Trumps and Courts. He employed artist Pamela Colman Smith, another Golden Dawn initiate, to execute them according to his instructions. Waite tried to reconcile Etteilla's interpretations of each card with those supplied by the Golden Dawn, not always an easy task! However, Waite's deck has succeeded over the past century in becoming the prototype for most of today's divinatory Tarot decks.

As for methods of spreading the cards for Tarot divination, there are today innumerable versions to choose from. Each diviner will have his or her own favorites. It has been my experience that any method can produce results, provided you approach the cards in the right frame of mind, that is, with respect and due seriousness. The rules and spreads that are contained in the "Little White Book" (LWB to Tarot fans) that generally accompanies every divinatory deck are perhaps as good as any. After many years of consulting the cards off and on, I have come to the conclusion that the ultimate secret of successful Tarot divination lies not in the cards, but within the card reader, in his or her own deep mind. The cards require interpretation, and the interpretations offered by the LWBs, traditional or not, are ultimately only scaffolding on which to hang your own intuition, which is something you acquire over a period of time and with much trial and error. The cards provide wonderful archetypal, highly evocative symbols which are, in effect, medieval mirrors of ourselves and all the conditions we find ourselves subjected to.

– Paul Huson

Paul Huson's latest book is Mystical Origins of the Tarot, *Destiny Books, Rochester, Vermont.*

The Sun as the Main Movable Star, from a 15th-century Italian tarocchi *deck.*

ORPHEUS AND EURYDICE

In the realm of silence and uncreated things

CONSIDER MUSIC as magic. So did the ancient Greeks consider the art in the most exquisitely vivid way. They conceived of Orpheus, son of Apollo, god of music, and of the muse Calliope, known as Beautiful Voice. The offspring of such dazzling parents played the lyre to such effect that nothing could withstand its enchantment. His song could stop tigers in their tracks, move trees to gather where he played, and melt rocks.

The melodies of Orpheus also melted the heart of the nymph Eurydice, and the couple loved each other with passion beyond description. Hymenaeus, the god of marriage, presided over their wedding, but accidentally bore them misfortune. His torch smoked and brought tears to the eyes of the bride and groom, a dark omen. And during the honeymoon, tragedy struck. On a dewy morning, as Eurydice played with her companions, a nearby shepherd was bowled over by her beauty. He rushed toward the nymph with coarse words, and as she fled Eurydice trod on a snake unseen in the tall grass. The serpent bit her foot, killing her.

Overcome by grief, Orpheus sang the saddest music ever to mount the farthest reaches of the sky. The song reached the ears of gods to no avail. Finally the heartbroken bridegroom resolved to seek his beloved in the abode of the dead. With the power of his nine-stringed lyre defending him from guardian perils and swarms of rustling ghosts, Orpheus descended into the Stygian realm.

The sound of sorrow

He stood before the ebony throne of Hades and the amethyst throne of Persephone and sang: "O deities of the underworld, to whom all we who live must come, hear my words, for they are true. I come to seek my wife, whose opening years the poisonous viper's fang has brought to an untimely end. Love has led me here, Love, a god all powerful with us who dwell on earth, and, if old traditions say true, not less so here. I implore you by these abodes full of terror, these realms of silence and uncreated things, unite again the thread of Eurydice's life. We are all destined to you, and sooner or later must pass to your domain. She too, when she shall have filled her term of life, will rightly be yours. But until then grant her to me, I beseech you. If you deny one, I cannot return alone; you shall triumph in the death of us both." As heart-cracked Orpheus sang these words, according to the mythologist Bulfinch, "the very ghosts shed tears."

Toward the air aboveground

Hades of the steely heart remained unmoved, for it is a condition of he who receives all, The Rich One, that no subject leave his somber realm. But the song of Orpheus even wet the cheeks of the Furies, and similarly effected Persephone. She pleaded to restore the life of Eurydice. Hades could not resist his beloved queen and summoned the nymph, who limped in on her injured foot. "You may take her away on one condition," Hades told Orpheus. "You may not look at her until you reach the air aboveground."

Orpheus led, Eurydice followed, winding the dark, steep trek upward. Now he heard the patter of her footsteps near him, now the patter of her footsteps lagging. Was that Eurydice? An apparition? An aural hallucination? When Orpheus approached the light of the upper air, "he knew he must have faith and he could not have faith." In "Orpheus and Eurydice," the Polish poet Czeslaw Milosz beautifully interprets the legend at length and concludes:

Day was breaking. Shapes of
rock loomed up
Under the luminous eye of the
exit from the underground.
It happened as he expected.
He turned his head
And behind him on the path
was no one.

Sun. And sky. And in the sky
white clouds.
Only now everything cried to him:
Eurydice!
How will I live without you, my
consoling one!
But there was a fragrant scent of
herbs, the low humming of bees,
And he fell asleep with his cheek
on the sun-warmed earth.

From our new publication, Greek Gods in Love, *by Barbara Stacy. To read other stories from the book, visit our website www.TheWitchesAlmanac.com/greekgodsinlove.*

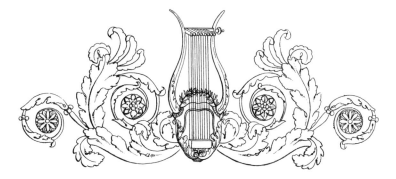

Buddha's Magical Numbers

Four Noble Truths – an Eightfold Path

IN OUR ACTION-DIRECTED world, most people think there's no point in sitting still. Modern witches, magicians and pagans might feel that we are more in touch with a slower, more cosmic rhythm – but are we? Even in metaphysical circles our lives may be overly busy, filled with daily obligations that seem to leave no time for calm reflection. For improved concentration, clearer connection to our inner selves and a deeper sense of compassion, one Buddhist teacher offers excellent advice: "Don't just do something, sit there!"

Although in the West we think of Buddhism as a religion, it is essentially a technique for understanding our essential nature and ending suffering. Substitute the phrase "true will" for "essential nature" and you will begin to see that the traditions of East and West might not be so far apart. In Greece, the famous inscription at the temple of Delphi advised, "Know thyself." The journey of the Buddha, Siddhartha Gautama, followed just that directive. Through the technique of sitting meditation he attained four insights, now called "The Four Noble Truths," and an "Eightfold Path" – fundamentals of every form of Buddhism worldwide.

The Noble Truths:

1. Nothing lasts forever. Expecting to be miserable when things come to an end. This is called "impermanence," often stated as "life is suffering."

2. This suffering starts because we are attached to the idea that things will last forever or that if we can just find the magic formula, we can make things the way want them to be, always. This is called "craving" or "attachment."

3. We don't have to be miserable. We can teach ourselves to let go of our cravings and attachments so that we don't have to suffer as much when things change, as they inevitably will. This truth is called "freedom from confinement" or "extinction." It is like getting the key to our jail cell or blowing out a candle burning us.

4. There is a path to liberation from suffering and getting burned by our expectations. This path runs between the extremes of hedonism and asceticism.

The Eightfold Path: Right Understanding, Right Intention, Right Speech, Right Action, Right Livelihood, Right Effort, Right Mindfulness, Right Concentration.

Meditation techniques

In the Buddhist view, the way to work on these techniques must be grounded in meditation, the eighth branch of the Path. Through sitting still, bringing full attention to what transpires mentally, a practitioner comes to understand how to embody the other parts of the path and attain freedom. When you temporarily remove the distractions of a busy life, you come to see how reactive your mind really is. It is quite shocking to realize how many activities you do almost in your sleep.

The basic technique given to Buddhist students is to simply sit, for perhaps five minutes a day in the beginning, just being aware of your breath as it moves in and out of your body. Thoughts seem to fill your every moment, demanding that you do their bidding. *Get up! What are you doing here, doing nothing? Feed the kids! Pay the bills! Did you remember to turn off the stove? Maybe the house is on fire. Go look. Get up! Get up!* You might think of this as "getting on the train."

Whenever you find yourself on the train, get off without adding more thoughts to the baggage. Like the demons that wrestled with the Buddha in his quest to awaken, your thoughts wrestle you. The impressions might get darker, scarier, more intense, but still, just get off the train. Keep going back to noticing your breath, a simple act always in the present moment.

After a long period of awareness about how many "worry, scurry" concerns race around, you begin to notice their ebbing. Perhaps you're not entirely made up of anxiety, anger and obligation. When fears begin to recede, detachment begins. This is when meditation becomes fruitful. You learn how to let go of disparaging attitudes toward yourself and others, and compassion springs up like grass after the rain. Anger, greed and ignorance loosen their grip. The negative actions of others seem less important and the small everyday moments in life are revealed as beautiful. You focus more on making better choices and forgiving yourself for mistakes. You are no longer a prisoner of your thoughts.

If you devote yourself firmly to this process, a deeper connection to life emerges. In this awareness lie the seeds of enlightenment or awakening – "Buddha" simply means "one who is awake." How do we assess a spiritual or religious path unless it makes us more compassionate, more grounded, focused and aware? If your personal path seems to be lacking these elements lately, you might want to try just sitting there.

– ELIZABETH ROSE

From Ming dynasty porcelain: the "eight Buddhist symbols"

Speaking of Witchcraft...
Cunning Folk, Hedge Witches, Night Travelers

"OLD CRAFT," "Traditional Craft," "Cunning Arts" – these terms don't spring to mind when we talk about witchcraft today. These arts are quite different from what we commonly refer to as the practice of Wicca, a word derived from witchcraft authority Gerald Gardner. He originally wrote the term spelled as "Wica," and defined it as a Celtic revivalist mystery religion. Gardner claimed that it was based on the practices of a coven of witches from the New Forest area of England. But for us today it is meaningful to understand the roots from older survivals of craft practice, which we call Old Craft and Traditional Craft.

Historically there were both solitary practitioners and those who gathered with others of their kind in what they called a "covine" or "cuveen." Cunning Men and Cunning Women were known throughout the countryside, and as late as the late nineteenth century some provided regular service of curing and cursing. Some of their Cunning Arts practices still prevail in British country life today as folkloric survivals and seasonal festivities.

The Cunning Folk who practiced this old craft were dispensers of popular superstition and collectors of arcane and esoteric lore. The charms and curios of their craft derived as often from the Far East as they did from local sources. Often they retained dual faith practices, a mixture of both the older pagan and newer Christian beliefs.

Hedge Craft is another form of Old Craft and practitioners of this variant are known as "Hedge Witches." This term derives from the Saxon word for witch, *haegtessa*, which translates to "Hedge Rider," and they are also known as "Night Travelers" and "Walkers on the Wind." In its more traditional sense, Hedge Witches are those who engage in spirit flight and journey into the Otherworld. And here we see the origins of some dismaying images of the witch, often viewed as uncanny and dangerous. In old village life, hedges stood on the boundary between the town and the wild areas. Passing beyond that boundary was dangerous; a natural fear of the unknown prevailed in that act. The witch often lived on that boundary or just beyond it. Villagers who desired the services of a Hedge Witch had to pluck up plenty of courage for the risky journey to her hearth!

– OWEN ROWLEY

Rasputin

The mad mystic

Grigory Rasputin surrounded by admirers

VILLAGERS IN HIS native Siberia predicted a bad end for their local wild boy. As a youth he enjoyed outraging authorities by diligence only in drunkenness, theft and lechery. His sexual appetite was legendary and Grigory Yefimovich Novykh became known as Rasputin, "the debauched one." But at age eighteen he shocked the community by joining a Russian Orthodox monastery. There Rasputin lingered for three months and found exactly what suited his tastes. Within its cloistered walls he discovered the Khlysts, a sect of flagellants. Adherents believed that the way to reach God was through prodigious sexual debauchery that left all passion spent; holiness lay in lack of desire. For the rest of his life Rasputin preached the doctrine of holy lechery and practiced what he preached.

Rasputin adapted the robes of a monk, which he was not, and assumed the guise of a *starets*, a self-proclaimed holy man who could heal through prayer and predict the future. He wandered Russia, journeyed to Greece and Jerusalem, and returned to make a stir with the peasants, whose donations supported him. Rasputin's increasing fame began to impress the Russian clergy; the Orthodox fathers were completely taken in by the charismatic *starets*. Inevitably he headed for the capital city, St. Petersburg.

Right place, right time

Rasputin's village wife and four children had long vanished from his program. In 1903, at the age of thirty-four, he arrived in the right place at the right time. Court ladies were entertaining themselves with a fad for the occult and Rasputin offered the ultimate package – mysticism laced with orgiastic sex. A glance at historical photos provide little clue to his appeal. His face was consumed by a bushy beard, his hair was scant and unkempt, and he was notoriously filthy. But Rasputin had a brilliant gaze and apparently projected no lack of charisma. Celebrity flourished and two years later he was introduced to the royal family.

Tsar Nicholas II and Alexandra adored each other, delighting more in domesticity than reign. The couple

particularly enjoyed the coziness of teatime with their four little daughters, happiness marred only by the lack of a son. The absence of an heir had become an obsession. At the birth of a boy in 1908, the royal family rejoiced. But within a month dark news issued from the nursery. The little prince was a victim of hemophilia, inherited through Alexandra's grandmother, Queen Victoria. The slightest bruise caused painful, persistent bleeding sometimes ending in death.

When Alexis was one year old, he suffered from a serious episode. His hysterical mother had lost trust in doctors and summoned Rasputin. The *starets* put a stop to the bleeding of the suffering little prince, then and in later attacks. Historians have speculated about these treatments for a hundred years – perhaps Rasputin indeed had mystical powers, perhaps he had mastered hypnotic technique. But to the devout parents, the *starets* was a holy gift from God, and Alexandra especially doted on her son's savior. Now Rasputin secured a lock on influence over the Romanovs that lasted nearly a decade.

Speeding the downfall

Russian subjects knew nothing of the prince's condition, and St. Petersburg society failed to understand the slovenly monk's intimacy with the royal family. His drunken parties and lechery had become so notorious that former supporters shunned him and became enemies. The city was rife with gossip about Rasputin, with rumors that included Alexandra, and fearful of his growing power. When World War I broke out Nicholas – with no military experience and ears deaf to counsel – left the capital to lead the troops, a disastrous move. He left Alexandra, who was even more obtuse than her husband, in charge of government affairs. Another disastrous move. Alexandra ran Russia, but Rasputin certainly ran Alexandra. He prevailed on the empress to dismiss capable ministers unfriendly to him and replaced them with nonentities or outright crooks. Ruinous changes occurred on a scale so pervasive that they seriously undermined the authority of the dynasty. Nicholas and Alexandra were doomed.

Cream cakes, Madeira, cyanide

The Russian aristocracy had more than enough of Rasputin. Three conspirators headed by the tsar's nephew, Prince Youssoupov, offered to introduce the monk to the prince's wife Irina, a famous beauty – the ultimate conquest. Rasputin rose to the bait. On December 29, 1916, he arrived at the Youssoupov palace at eleven o'clock. The menu for the guest of honor included wine and tea cakes liberally laced with cyanide. That night Rasputin consumed enough poison "to kill a horse" without showing any particular ill effect. He kept on chatting, drank more wine, and finally admitted to "feeling uncomfortable." But waiting for Irina, he drank more wine and sang raucous songs until two in the morning.

Eventually the unnerved accomplices realized that Rasputin seemed immune to poison. They would just have to shoot him. One shot had him down but not out. Rasputin staggered into the courtyard, where he was shot two more times, once in the head. Still he lived! The assassins were terrified at this show of superhuman strength. They wrapped him in a carpet and dragged him to a nearby canal running into the Neva. The killers chopped a hole in the ice and threw in their victim. Three days later his frozen body was found, drowning the cause of death.

The aristocracy was enraptured. But the peasants considered Rasputin "one of their own," revered him as a holy man, and wept for his passing. His murder provided another reason to loathe the elite. Three months later a Bolshevik firing squad abolished Russian royalty forever.

– BARBARA COBELL

Hsi Wang Mu

Queen Mother of Western Paradise

HSI WANG MU *(shee-wang-myu)* reigns as one of the most poetic goddesses in the universal pantheon. To the Chinese she represents the feminine principle of yin; her spouse, Mu Gong, is the complementary masculine yang. Together the primal couple engendered heaven, earth, and all living things.

The goddess is depicted as ravishingly beautiful, wearing royal finery and riding a peacock or phoenix. She is the deity of Taoist priestesses and adepts, appearing in dreams and visions, protecting adherents. Hsi Wang Mu and her consort live in a nine-story jade palace in the misty heavens of the Kun-lun mountains. Violet clouds form its dome, blue clouds form its walls, the lustrous Lake of Turquoise laps its shores. The palace is surrounded by a fence of pure gold a thousand miles long. Hsi Wang Mu has dominion over the female genies or spirits inhabiting the Garden of West Flower, while her husband dominates East Flower. Her fairyland paradise abounds in rare blooms, exotic birds, and the magical flat peach, *p'an-t'ao.*

The Immortal Peach Tree
Hsi Wang Mu's garden provides the Peaches of Immortality, which ripen every three thousand years on the deity's birthday. Hsi Wang Mu offers a grand banquet to celebrate the occasion. The guests are the Eight Immortals who reside in the jade palace, male spirits in the right wing, female spirits in the left. The menu includes odd delicacies: bear claws, monkey lips, dragon livers. Excitement reaches fever pitch at the dessert. Beneath the fuzzy skin that puckers the mouth lies the pale flesh of the West Flower peach; sweet, juicy, transcendental. Eternal magic reinforced. Sometimes during the party Hsi Wang Mu and the Immortals become drunk on the fragrance of paradise and on *t'ien chiu,* heavenly wine.

We know little about the Eight Immortals, but we do know about Ho Hsien-ku, her beauty enhanced with lotus adornments in lieu of jewels. She dreamed as a young girl that mother-of-pearl conferred immortality. Nibbling a bit of shell, Ho Hsien-ku morphed into an ethereal creature floating across the hills. She spent her days gathering herbs, gliding back to the palace at night with her harvest. Fifty years later villagers marveled at sightings of Ho Hsien-ku hovering among the clouds.

Han Hsiang, another of the Eight, declared that he could make flowers bloom at will. His uncle scoffed at such a crazy claim, so Han Hsiang instantly created a clod of earth springing with glorious flowers. To add to the marvel, a poem of fourteen golden characters embellished the leaves. As for Immortal Chang Kuo-lao, artists depict him holding a magical peach and a phoenix feather. He sits backwards riding a marvelous mule that folds up like paper when not needed.

White Tigress, Golden Tortoise, Divine Gardener

The highest goddess in the Taoist religion began her mythological life improbably. She emerged from ancient times as the White Tigress, described in a text written before 2000 B.C. Here Hsi Wang Mu is depicted as a mountain spirit with a tiger's teeth and the tail of a leopard. Three bluebirds provide her food and carry her messages. According to the ancient manual, the White Tigress revealed the sexual and spiritual refinements of *ching* (sexual energy), *chi* (vital energy) and *shen* (consciousness), said to provide eternal youthfulness and immortality. White Tiger disciplines were practiced by a long line of courtesans and women Taoists; vestiges of the tradition still exist in Asia, particularly in Taiwan. In a later form Hsi Wang Mu turns up as Mother of the Golden Tortoise, an identity with a whiff of sorcery that encompasses turtle-shell divination.

With the advent of Taoism, Hsi Wang Mu assumed her final form as the highest goddess in the pantheon, the feminine element itself. The divinity achieved enormous popularity, particularly among women outside the roles of "dutiful daughter, obedient wife, and self-sacrificing mother." Hsi Wang Mu, independent and powerful, bestowed inspiration on novices and nuns; the only women allowed literacy. The goddess was also served by the Jade Maidens, skilled in music, poetry and sexuality. These celestial attendants provided models for women performers, musicians and especially brothel singers.

The concept of sexual freedom aroused plenty of consternation among the yang sector. According to one medieval text, "The Queen of the Western Paradise has no husband but she liked to copulate with young boys. The secret, however, should not be divulged, lest other women should try to imitate the Queen Mother's methods." Sassy women, and goddesses as well, seem to have inspired slander down the ages.

Should you want to celebrate the next Immortal Peach feast along with the Queen Mother of Western Paradise, we can't be encouraging. The occasion doesn't arise again until the year 5078.

– Barbara Stacy

The Night of the Watchers
June 5

SINCE its very first issue *The Witches' Almanac* has always commemorated the Night of the Watchers, which falls on June 5. But who are these Watchers and what is their Night? And why does it fall on June 5?

Only brief answers to these questions can be found in *The Witches' Almanac*. In the Almanac for 1973-74, the Watchers were briefly defined as "the sleepless ones or 'fallen angels' of Hebrew Legend who mated with the daughters of men to whom they taught the forbidden arts."

Three decades had to pass before readers of *The Witches' Almanac* could find out more about the Watchers. The

Almanac for 2004/5 devoted a single page to their legend as it is found in the apocryphal *Book of Enoch*. (See our article about the *Book of Enoch* on page 108 in this issue of the Almanac.) That page ended with the sentences, "the tale of the Watchers was popular during the Middle Ages. Their arrival date of June 5 was noted on calendar manuscripts of the period."

In reply to a question of mine about this date, Elizabeth Pepper said that she had taken it on trust from another person when she was putting together the very first issue *The Witches' Almanac* in 1970 or 1971. In fact, she seems to have been the very first person to give any date for the Night of the Watchers. I have not been able to find any mention of that event in any known calendar or almanac, nor any precise date given for it in any work on chronology.

Indeed, there does not appear to be any ancient esoteric or occult lore of any kind about June 5. The only mention of the date that I have found in any speculative context is quite recent. In 1954 a German engineer named Otto Heinrich Muck published a book, *Atlantis – gefunden (Atlantis Found)*, in which he argued that Atlantis had been destroyed by the fall of an asteroid precisely on June 5 in the year 8498 BC. This date, he claimed, was also the zero-day from which the ancient Mayan calendar counted all its days and its years. He also pointed out that 8498 BC agreed roughly with Plato's vague reference to the time of the destruction of Atlantis, and also with a vague mention by Herodotus of the time when the first of 345 generations of gigantic priests had begun to serve Amun in his temple at Thebes. Before that year, so Herodotus reported, Egypt had been ruled not by giants, but by gods.

Specialists in the study of Mayan civilization no longer regard either the year 8498 BC or the date June 5 as the true starting-point for Mayan calendar calculations. Even in Muck's own time, only a few scholars argued for a starting-point in that year, and they wrote only of an undetermined date in early June, not June 5 precisely. Muck appears to have settled on June 5 because it was also the date of a triple conjunction between the Sun, the Moon and Venus in that year, and he supposed that the combined gravitational forces of these three bodies could have deflected an asteroid from its orbit as it passed near the outer planet, causing it to fall to earth with cataclysmic force.

In 1954, too, a French humanist named Denis Saurat published a speculative book, *L'Atlantide et le règne des géants* (*Atlantis and the Reign of the Giants*), which linked the destruction of Atlantis to the legend of Watchers and their giant offspring, and also to the rise of advanced civilizations in the lands around the Atlantic and the Mediterranean.

Although Muck's work was not translated into English until 1978, his views were certainly known before that date to many authors who were writing about Atlantis, as were Saurat's. (An English version of Saurat's book had appeared in 1957.) Somewhere in the vast sea of books and articles on Atlantis that were written in English between 1954 and 1970 there should be at least one work in which Muck's date for the destruction of Atlantis was combined with Saurat's account of the role of the Watchers and the giants to yield the conclusion that June 5 marked the day of their departure from Atlantis and their arrival in the lands around the Atlantic Ocean. This work would be the ultimate source of the idea that June 5 was when the Watchers descended from heaven and first instructed men and women in forbidden knowledge.

– ROBERT MATHIESEN

Crystal Balls

Visions in smoke

WE'VE ALL SEEN the image of the fortune teller with her headscarf, peasant blouse, broomstick skirt. Her fingers are covered with rings, her forearms decked with gold bracelets. She sits at a round table passing her hands in circular motions over a ball. A client may be listening to her say, "I see a tall, dark stranger..." Perhaps you've wondered if you too could see visions in a crystal ball.

The process begins with the right material. Many balls are now made of acrylic and much more affordable than the traditional quartz crystal. Whatever material you choose, select your crystal carefully to make sure it is free of scratches, bubbles, or occlusions. Use the crystal in a darkened room. The only light should be a candle, positioned so that the flame does not reflect in the ball. Bring yourself into a relaxed state and gaze at the ball. Blink naturally. Clear your mind.

After a time the ball will appear to fill with smoke and then gradually clear, leaving behind a scene. Allow your mind to make free associations. Note the spatial relationships and movement of images. Ascending clouds are believed to answer questions in the affirmative; descending, negative.

You may not see anything at first. Try passing your hands over the ball. Passes with the right give power, while passes with the left increase your sensitivity to the crystal's messages. If you do not see anything after ten minutes, put the ball away and try again later. Even with daily practice it may take as much as a week to see something.

When the ball is not in use, swaddle it in silk or velvet and store it away. Some crystal gazers feel that only the owner should handle the mystical ball. Other adepts have the querent hold the ball and meditate on a question.

If you're not sure you want to invest in a crystal ball, try one of the traditional substitutes – a mirror, a bowl of ink, or even a dark bowl of water. Practice gazing as described above. Be patient. Sooner or later you have a good chance of encountering visions in smoke.

– MORVEN WESTFIELD

The MOON Calendar

is divided into zodiac signs rather than the more familiar Gregorian calendar.

2008

2009

Bear in mind that new projects should be initiated when the Moon is waxing (from dark to full); when the Moon is on the wane (from full to dark), it is a time for storing energy and the wise person waits.

Please note that Moons are listed by day of entry into each sign. Quarters are marked, but as rising and setting times vary from one region to another, it is advisable to check your local newspaper, library or planetarium.
The Moon's Place is computed for Eastern Standard Time.

∽ The Enigmatic Egg ∽

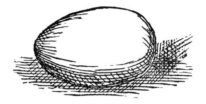

A POWERFUL ELEMENT of spells around the world, the egg is a beloved and mysterious symbol. A food source, believed an aphrodisiac and a token of new life, as a famous riddle suggests the egg is a true "golden treasure in a box without lid or key."

In spring traditions worldwide, colored eggs welcome the awakening sun's return. Ancient Egyptians believed that the god Ptah emerged from an egg laid by the Chaos Goose, possibly the origin of Mother Goose. In Eastern Orthodox tradition eggs are decorated with the letters XB to honor Christ's rising after death, another new-life metaphor. Russians greet each other with gifts of decorative eggs, and for the rich, jeweled Fabergé eggs expanded on this custom. In Poland intricate Easter eggs called *pysanky* are vivid with colored wax. Their designs originate in the belief that the Virgin Mary made them to please the baby Jesus.

As fertility efforts, European peasants rubbed a paste of eggs, bread and flour on newly plowed land, hoping to improve the harvest. French brides cracked eggs on the doorsteps of their new homes to assure a large family. In China newborn babies are gifted with red eggs for luck.

The Easter Bunny, who delivers baskets of eggs and other treats to children, originally sprang from a German tradition. The prolific bunny is another emblem of renewal and vitality.

– ESTHER ELAYNE

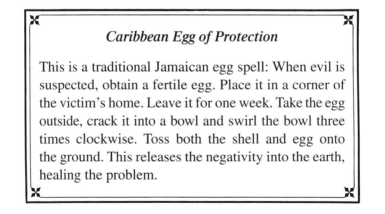

Caribbean Egg of Protection

This is a traditional Jamaican egg spell: When evil is suspected, obtain a fertile egg. Place it in a corner of the victim's home. Leave it for one week. Take the egg outside, crack it into a bowl and swirl the bowl three times clockwise. Toss both the shell and egg onto the ground. This releases the negativity into the earth, healing the problem.

aries

March 20 – April 19

Cardinal Sign of Fire △ Ruled by Mars ♂

S	M	T	W	T	F	S
				MAR. 20 2008 Vernal Equinox Virgo	21 (Seed Moon) Libra	22 Waning *Heavy rains will fall*
23	24 *Harry Houdini born, 1874* Scorpio	25 *Stop a bad habit*	26 Sagittarius	27	28	29 ◑ Capricorn
30	31 Aquarius	APRIL 1 All Fools Day	2 *Catch a falling feather*	3 Pisces	4 *Whisper a wish*	5 ● Aries
6 Waxing	7 *Bless seeds* Taurus	8	9 *Follow an honest path* Gemini	10	11 *Plant seeds indoors* Cancer	12 ◑
13 *Thomas Jefferson born, 1743* Leo	14 *Trust a gypsy*	15 *Control your temper*	16 Virgo	17	18 *Change a color* Libra	19

Illustration by Ogmios MacMerlin

YEAR OF THE EARTH RAT
February 7, 2008 to January 26, 2009

Respected in the Orient for craftiness and charm, Rat's attributes also include tenaciousness and diligence. When the world was young, Rat persuaded good-natured Ox to let him ride on Ox's back to answer a summons from Buddha. As they approached the Holy One, Rat jumped over Ox's head and managed to arrive at Buddha's feet first. Impressed, Buddha gifted Rat with the first sign in the oldest of the world's zodiacs.

Years of the Rat are considered auspicious, favoring creativity, innovation, and liberal philosophies. Prosperity is indicated, and a propitious time prevails to seek collectibles. Many will experience a closer attunement with nature and a successful pursuit of ecological concerns.

Oriental astrology follows a cycle of twelve years, named in honor of the twelve animals that attended the Buddha. Each animal is said to reside in the hearts of those born under their sign. The cycle also incorporates five elements – fire, water, wood, metal, and earth. Each sixty years the element/animal pairs repeat.

If you were born during one of the Years of the Rat, as listed below, you will be starting a new cycle of growth and opportunity this year. Scurry to make the most of the great opportunities that are about to present themselves!

1912   1924   1936   1948   1960   1972   1984   1996   2008

taurus

April 20 – May 20

Fixed Sign of Earth ▽ Ruled by Venus ♀

S	M	T	W	T	F	S
APRIL 20 **Hare Moon** Scorpio	21 Waning	22	23 Find a rainbow Sagittarius	24	25 Capricorn	26 John James Audubon born, 1785
27	28 Aquarius	29	30 Beltane Eve Pisces	MAY 1 Roodmas ✠ Dance the Maypole	2 Aries	3
4 Turn a coin Taurus	5	6 Waxing Gemini	7 Plan your garden	8 White Lotus Day Cancer	9 Good planting day	10 Leo
11	12 Face a challenge Virgo	13	14	15 Libra	16 Knot green thread for luck	17 Scorpio
18	19 **Flower Moon**	20 Waning Socrates born, 469 BCE Sagittarius				

31

Reading the Ribbons

IN TIMES PAST, women considered ribbons, laces and braid trims treasures too pretty ever to discard. Among the mystical traditions of Western Europe, especially in Scotland, a kitchen-witch custom developed around bright ribbon bundles. The ribbons were knotted or stitched together at one end, then used as a form of divination. Those who came to seek advice from the wise one would be invited to select a ribbon. The reader would then combine psychometry with intuition to weave a story apropos to the situation. Today with the popularity of tarot, palmistry, mediumship and other divination systems on the rise, ribbon reading can again be enjoyed as a simple, beautiful and comfortable way to both divine the future and understand the past.

Begin with seven ribbons, saved, given or purchased, but carefully selected. Seven is a number associated with wisdom. Think of the seven chakras in the body; the Sun, Moon and visible planets are seven. There are seven musical notes, seven days of the week, seven archangels, and other seven relationships. As time passes, more lovely ribbons may come your way and they can be added to the original bundle. Any length is fine, but bundles about two feet long work well. They are attractive set on a reading table and not too unwieldy to handle.

The reader can either pre-assign a meaning to a ribbon or thoughtfully consider what it means to a specific situation as questions arise. For example, a lace can relate to memories and history, while a ribbon embellished with snowflakes can indicate a change as winter nears. A vibrant, rich red ribbon suggests success and quality. Cheerful fringe hints at travel to a sunny climate and a holiday. The possibilities are endless. With a little practice, the wisdom carried in the ribbon bundle will unravel to reveal new depths of understanding.

– MARINA BRYONY

gemini

May 21 – June 20

Mutable Sign of Air ♎ Ruled by Mercury ☿

S	M	T	W	T	F	S
			May 21	22	23 *Give a gift of colored glass*	24 *Bob Dylan born, 1941*
				Capricorn		
25	26 *Study the birds*	27 ◑	28 *The wind gives a message*	29 Oak Apple Day	30	31
Aquarius		Pisces			Aries	
June 1	2	3 ●	4 Waxing *Walk barefoot in the grass*	5 Night of the Watchers	6	7
Taurus		Gemini		Cancer		Leo
8	9 *Johnny Depp born, 1963*	10 ◐	11 Hang wind chimes	12 Anne Frank born, 1929	13	14
	Virgo		Libra			Scorpio
15 *Tea with the fairies*	16	17 Vesak Day ⇨ (Buddha's Birthday)	18 ◯ Dyad Moon	19 Waning Midsummer Eve	20 Summer Solstice ☼	
Sagittarius				Capricorn		

33

The Bald Man and the Fly

Aesop's Fables   Illustrated by Arthur Rackham

THE WAS ONCE a Bald Man who sat down after work on a hot summer's day. A Fly came up and kept buzzing about his bald pate, and stinging him from time to time. The Man aimed a blow at his little enemy, but – whack – his palm came on his head instead; again the Fly tormented him, but this time the Man was wiser and said:

"You will only injure yourself if you take notice of despicable enemies."

cancer

June 21 – July 22

Cardinal Sign of Water ▽ Ruled by Moon ☽

S	M	T	W	T	F	S
						JUNE 21 Jean-Paul Sartre born, 1905 Aquarius
22 Gather St. John's Wort	**23** Pisces	**24**	**25** Consult the Runes	**26** ◑ Aries	**27**	**28** Taurus
29	**30** Ask a seer Gemini	**JULY 1** Princess Diana born, 1961	**2** ● Cancer	**3** Waxing Carry a charm	**4** Leo	**5**
6 Virgo	**7**	**8** Gather shells Libra	**9** ◐	**10**	**11** Hold fast to romance Scorpio	**12**
13 Sagittarius	**14**	**15** Avoid fire	**16** Fashion a poppet Capricorn	**17**	**18** ◯ Mead Moon	**19** Waning Aquarius
20	**21** Walk by the sea Pisces	**22**				

Nostradamus and the Pigs

THE SIXTEENTH-CENTURY prophet generally predicted war, death, natural disasters – monumental events he augured primarily through astrological calculations. But lovers of Nostradamus cherish the little story of the farmer, the white pig and the black pig.

Nostradamus was invited to a feast by a rich farmer, skeptical of the prophet's abilities. The farmer had two pigs ready to serve his guests, he told Nostradamus, a white pig and a black pig. Which would be presented at dinner?

"The black pig," Nostradamus replied.

The farmer went into the kitchen and ordered the chef to serve the white pig.

During the course of the feast the farmer summoned his chef and asked which pig the guests were consuming. "When my back was turned a dog carried off the carcass of the white pig," he confessed. "So I served the black pig."

The story happens to be true but sounds like a fable. The moral might be: Seers may see large and seers may see small.

leo

July 23 – August 22
Fixed Sign of Fire △ Ruled by Sun ☉

LEO

S	M	T	W	T	F	S
			JULY 23 Ancient Egyptian New Year Aries	24	25 Taurus	26
27 Gemini	28	29 Cancer	30 Bake bread	31 Total ⇨ solar eclipse Lughnassad Eve	AUGUST 1 Lammas Leo	2 Waxing
3 Virgo	4 Trust the Tarot	5 Libra	6 Sing a song	7 Mata Hari born, 1876 Scorpio	8	9
10 Patience pays off Sagittarius	11	12 Helena Blavatsky born, 1831 Capricorn	13 Diana's Day	14 Avoid over-indulgence	15 Full Moon partial lunar eclipse ⇨ Aquarius	16 Wort Moon
17 Waning Pisces	18 Less can be more	19 Aries	20 Blessings hide in shadows	21 Taurus	22	

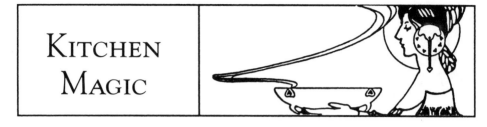

KITCHEN MAGIC

Glorious peaches

PEACHES, ROSY, BRIMMING with juice, are one of the glories of summertime. In their native China peaches symbolize longevity, and to give a friend a ceramic image of the fruit indicates great esteem. From China peaches made their way through Persia and into India, my own Asian background. I love peaches, prepared unripe, teamed with ginger and chile pepper and made into a flavorful chutney, delicious with broiled fish. My American favorite is classic Peach Cobbler, an individual one-crust pastry that never grew up into a pie.

To remove their fuzzy overcoats, blanch peaches: Dip them for 30 seconds into boiling water and plunge them into ice water. Skins will slip off readily.

Ginger Peach Chutney
2 pounds green or unripe peaches
2 cloves garlic, minced
4 tablespoons olive oil
1 teaspoon salt
1 green serrano chile, finely chopped
juice of 2 fresh lemons
1 teaspoon grated ginger

Peel peaches, shred them on the shredder side of a grater, and combine all ingredients. Turn into a container and store in the refrigerator. Serve with broiled fish.

Peach Cobbler
2 lbs. ripe peaches (preferably vine ripened)
2/3 cup light brown sugar
1/4 teaspoon lime zest

Crust:
1 cup flour
3 tablespoons butter
3 tablespoons buttermilk
beaten egg

Peel and remove pits and core from peaches. Cut them into 1/4- or 1/2-inch slices. Toss them with the sugar and lime peel and divide the mixture into six 3- to 4-inch-wide baking dishes.

Combine crust ingredients into a dough and knead lightly. Flatten the dough with your hand and chill for 30 minutes or until firm. Cut it into rings with a glass or mug and place the rounds on top of the peaches. With a pastry brush, brush the pastry with a little beaten egg. Bake in a 375° F oven for 35 to 45 minutes, until the crust is nicely brown. Serve warm with vanilla ice cream or whipped cream.

Hsi Wang Mu and her sacred party guests (page 22 in this issue) enjoyed "heavenly wine" with her immortal peaches. Wine lovers might emulate the goddess and enjoy a glass of "heavenly" aged reisling with the cobbler.

– SUNITA DUTT

virgo

August 23 – September 22

Mutable Sign of Earth ♍ Ruled by Mercury ☿

S	M	T	W	T	F	S
						Aug. 23 ◑
24 Gemini	25	26 Mother Teresa born, 1910 Cancer	27	28 Harvest herbs Leo	29	30 ● Virgo
31 Waxing	Sept. 1 Save apple seeds Libra	2	3 Ganesh Festival Scorpio	4 Forgive a hurt	5	6 Bless your familiar Sagittarius
7 ◖	8	9 Capricorn	10 Consult the Runes	11 Aquarius	12 Open a treasure box	13 Pisces
14 Carry Lapis Lazuli	15 Barley Moon	16 Waning Heed ancestor's wisdom Aries	17	18 Tend to magical wood Taurus	19	20 Gemini
21 Autumnal Equinox ♌	22 ◑ Cancer					

39

Hathor at Dendera

ON THE EDGE of the Egyptian desert lies the ancient city of Dendera. Behind the mud brick walls in this isolated area are a cluster of well-preserved temples from antiquity. The site was paramount to the worship of Hathor, the female deity par excellence in the earliest pantheon. Her temple rises magnificently from foundations that date to the fourth millennium. Hathor is most often associated with the Celestial Cow, one who protects calves, and in her motherly aspect safeguards pregnant women and children. The temple compound includes a birthing house. Hathor is depicted with cow's ears, as seen on the temple pillars, or horns cradling a sun disk.

The deity meant everything to women of the era. She is the patron of beauty, love, sexuality, joy, dance and music. Hathor enjoyed a large female priesthood performing during temple rituals as dancers, singers and musicians. At Dendera Hathor is also associated with the sistrum – a metal rattle thought to echo a papyrus stem being shaken. The sound was considered protective, symbolic of Hathor's divine blessings.

The goddess is known as Eye of the Sun, the daughter of Ra, and she dances to charm the sun god when he is in a stormy mood. In her fascinating Distant Goddess myth, Hathor clashes with Ra and wanders away from Egypt. Grief falls over the land and Ra, lost without his Eye, decides to fetch her. But the benevolent Hathor has turned feral, into a raging wildcat, and no one knows how to catch her. Thoth eventually manages to coax her home with stories, and back in Egypt she bathes in the Nile to calm the flames of rage. Eventually the waters cool Hathor down to her usual gentle demeanor, but not before the waters of the river turn red – emblematic of divine rage shed.

– LENURA BARD

libra

September 23 – October 22

Cardinal Sign of Air ♎ Ruled by Venus ♀

LIBRA

S	M	T	W	T	F	S
		Sept. 23	24	25	26	27
					Enjoy a confection	
			Leo		Virgo	
28	29	30	Oct. 1	2	3	4
Cleanse your home		Waxing		Mahatma Gandhi born, 1869	Write a friend	
		Rumi born, 1207				
	Libra		Scorpio		Sagittarius	
5	6	7	8	9	10	11
	Pick apples		Wear antique jewelry	Burn Juniper and wish		
	Capricorn		Aquarius			Pisces
12	13	14	15	16	17	18
	Give a passionate kiss	Blood Moon	Waning Gaze at the moon			Perform an augury
	Aries		Taurus		Gemini	
19	20	21	22			
			Study the stars			
Cancer		Leo				

Dark Moon Magic

WHY IS MAGIC WORK performed most often on nights of the full moon? Does the brighter light provide more energy to aid our spells? Does illumination equal energy? Perhaps not. Illumination allows for clarity of our desires, but the energy to make desires reality is the energy of the dark moon.

Darkness conjures up childhood fears. Is someone hiding in the bedroom closet? Things that are hidden or invisible feel scary. The witches of the past did not fear the dark. They understood the cycles of birth, death, and rebirth. They knew the secrets of the dark moon's power.

The dark moon begins at the end of the waning crescent and remains dark until the first hint of the waxing crescent. For those three days, the moon disappears into its dark phase. The first day of the dark is the remaining cycle of the waning moon. The second day, the moon hangs between dark and light. Then the first light is seen. In that time, between the end of the old moon and the advent of the new, a tremendous amount of energy builds.

Think of the amount of energy a seed that is germinating needs to push through the ground into the light. Once above, it effortlessly grows toward the sun. The same principle applies to the moon. To move from stillness to motion requires more power than continuation once the momentum has begun. As the moon waxes, the cycle is already in motion and the moon effortlessly seems to grow full. The change from dark to that first crescent of moonlight, however, requires more energy than at any other time in the cycle.

By choosing to work with the moon just past the nadir of its dark phase, workers in magic can use the growing energy to aid spells. Like a musical crescendo, as the light builds desires will be thrust out to the universe for all the gods to hear. Dark is a perfect beginning. It is empty and full of potential. In life if something is to be created, a space must first exist for desires to enter. When there is no light, a tremendous amount of space remains that can be filled with a desire.

Light is seen more clearly in darkness. The light of the stars is brightest during the dark moon. With a light sky, the stars are hardly visible. Aided by the energy of the dark moon and the power of all the stars, magic can be extremely successful.

Beginning a new project or coming up with a new way to solve a problem requires motivation and energy from within that cannot be seen. In the same way, when the moon is dark internal energy starts to build before the first sliver of light can be seen. Witches work with unseen energies all the time. Try tapping into the energies of the dark moon and see how its power can nourish your magical work.

– ANASTASIA C.

42

scorpio
October 23 – November 21
Fixed Sign of Water ▽ Ruled by Pluto ♀

S	M	T	W	T	F	S
				Oct. 23 Virgo	24	25
26 Libra	27 Captain Cook born, 1728	28 Scorpio	29 Waxing Assemble the spirits	30 Gather acorns Sagittarius	31 Samhain Eve	Nov. 1 Hallowmas
2 Daylight Savings Time ends at 2 a.m. Capricorn	3	4 A lucky day for twins	5 Aquarius	6	7 Express gratitude Pisces	8
9 Carl Sagan born, 1934 Aries	10 Visit a crossroads	11	12 Work with Moonstones Taurus	13 Snow Moon	14 Waning Keep mirrors clean Gemini	15
16 Hecate Night Cancer	17 Keep a watchful eye	18 Leo	19 Virgo	20	21	

43

TAROT'S JUSTICE

Rider-Waite-Smith deck

Card XI of the Major Arcana resonates with Libra. The scales suggest that elements will be balanced and right will prevail. All sides of an issue must be examined. Trivia will be pared away by the sword, the scales will be on an equal level, and only what is important remains to point toward truth. For those involved in legal concerns, the card emphasizes honesty and impartiality. The Justice card also deals with necessary adjustments pertaining to marriage or a partnership. On a less mundane level, Justice deals with responsibility, being accountable, doing whatever needs to be done, even if the right course is unpleasant. Again, the sword reminds us of difficult duty. Old accounts and debts require settling. One must accept the consequences of dubious behavior, then decide on right actions and set a scrupulously fair outcome for the future.

If Justice is reversed, it can indicate prejudice, legal obstruction or legal complications.

sagittarius

November 22 – December 20

Mutable Sign of Fire △ Ruled by Jupiter ♃

S	M	T	W	T	F	S
						Nov. 22 Libra
23	24 *Exercise caution twice!* Scorpio	25	26 *Thoughts manifest*	27 ● Sagittarius	28 Waxing	29 Capricorn
30	Dec. 1 *Challenges build strength*	2 *Observe clouds* Aquarius	3	4 *Heed an omen* Pisces	5 ◐	6 *Agnes Moorehead born, 1906*
7 Aries	8 *Contact a cherished friend*	9 Taurus	10	11 *Give a special gift* Gemini	12 Oak Moon	13 Waning *Bring holly indoors* Cancer
14 *Make wassail*	15 Leo	16 Fairy Queen Eve	17 Saturnalia Virgo	18 *Learn a riddle*	19 ◑ Libra	20 *Uri Geller born, 1946*

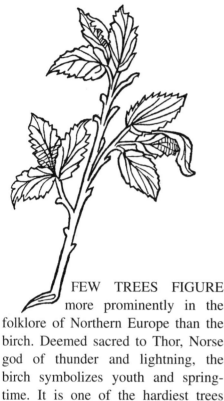

Birch

December 24 to January 20

FEW TREES FIGURE more prominently in the folklore of Northern Europe than the birch. Deemed sacred to Thor, Norse god of thunder and lightning, the birch symbolizes youth and springtime. It is one of the hardiest trees in the world; growing further north, and, with the rowan and the ash, higher up mountains than any other species. The birch is called "the tree of inception" with good reason. Not only does it self-sow, forming groves, but it is one of the earliest forest trees to put out leaves in spring.

An Old English folk-ballad titled *The Wife of Usher's Well* has a line: "And their hats were o' the birk," echoing a rural theme that souls returning from the dead decked themselves with branches plucked from the birth trees surrounding the gates of Paradise. The boughs were worn for protection lest the winds of Earth discover them and thwart their mission. Medieval art often depicts a ghostly presence as a figure arrayed in birch branches.

Its uncanny nature links the tree with witchcraft. Birch is the wood of broomsticks; flying transport to the sabbat gatherings. Oral tradition holds that witches anoint their birch rods with the words: "Away we go, not too high and not too low."

Siberian shamans may still seek the "magic mushroom" (the scarlet white-spotted fly agaric) in birch groves where it flourishes. Intoxicated by the ritually ingested mushrooms, shamans reach a state of ecstasy by climbing a birch tree and cutting nine notches in its crown.

Birch lore turns up in many cultures. The Dakota Sioux burn birch bark to discourage thunder spirits. Dutch farmers decorate a birch branch with red and white ribbons to safeguard horses in their stables. Scandinavians carry a young dried leaf for good luck on the first day of a new job. Basque witches use birch oil to anoint love candles. A bough on the roof protects a German home from lightning strikes. A birch grove guarded the house and land in colonial New England. Many sources claim that smoke rising from a fire of birch logs purifies the surroundings.

capricorn
December 21 – January 19
Cardinal Sign of Earth ▽ Ruled by Saturn ♄

S	M	T	W	T	F	S
Dec. 21 Winter Solstice ☉	22 *Call to* *the sun* *at sunrise* Scorpio	23	24 *Talk to* *animals* Sagittarius	25	26	27 ● Capricorn
28 Waxing	29 Aquarius	30 *Burn* *Bay Laurel*	31 *Prepare* *goals for* *coming year*	Jan. 1 2009 Pisces	2 *Catch a* *snowflake*	3 Aries
4 ◐	5 *Set a* *good* *example* Taurus	6 *Kahlil* *Gibran* *born, 1883*	7 Gemini	8	9 Feast of Janus Cancer	10 Wolf Moon
11 Waning Leo	12	13 Virgo	14 *Read* *your diary*	15	16 *Wear* *an amulet* Libra	17 ◑
18 Scorpio	19 *Forgive*					

Art of the Hedgehog

Observe which way the hedgehog builds her nest,
To front the north or south or east or west;
For if 'tis true what common people say,
The wind will blow the quite contrary way.

If by some secret art the hedgehog knows
So long before, the way in which the winds will blow,
She has an art which many a person lacks
That thinks himself fit to make our almanacks.

– 18th century American rhyme

aquarius

January 20 – February 18

Fixed Sign of Air ♎ Ruled by Uranus ♅

S	M	T	W	T	F	S
		Jan. 20 Sagittarius	21	22	23 Hold memories dear Capricorn	24 Welcome a stranger
25 Partial solar eclipse ⇨ Aquarius	26 **Year of the Ox**	27 Waxing New adventure	28 Pisces	29 The old feel young	30 Aries	31 Gone but not forgotten
Feb. 1 Oimelc Eve	2 ◐ Taurus	3 Candlemas ⇦	4 Rosa Parks born, 1913 Gemini	5	6 Watch and wait Cancer	7
8 Partial lunar eclipse ⇨ Leo	9 Storm Moon	10 Waning Ward off evil Virgo	11	12 Charles Darwin born, 1809 Libra	13	14 Don't delay Scorpio
15 Lupercalia	16 ◑	17 Hear the melody Sagittarius	18			

Edward Kelly

A Rascal and a Mystic

EDWARD KELLY (1555-1595) was an Irish alchemist and magician, his life a story of conflicting themes. He wore a cap to hide the fact that his ears had been cut off for committing forgery, yet he was also knighted by Emperor Rudolph II for his alchemical achievements in transmuting metals. Kelly was also later imprisoned by the Emperor for failing to deliver the promised alchemical gold and reputedly died trying to escape.

Kelly's most enduring contribution to the magical arts is his work with John Dee, the English Renaissance-era scientist and magician. Together they translated angelic transmissions from a poetic language called Enochian. Kelly, the visionary medium, used a crystal ball for long scrying sessions in which angelic spirits revealed to Kelly and John Dee many puzzling clues to arcane knowledge, including a system resembling ancient Gnostic cosmology. In these sessions, Kelly saw and spoke with an angelic intelligence that communicated in this unique language. At times the language was tapped out on a board, while at other times the language was delivered from the angelic spirits on strips of paper.

The spirits claimed that this language, Enochian, was the original speech of the Hebrew peoples, the language in which God spoke to Adam. With such a language, Dee and Kelly hoped arcane secrets would be revealed that would help conclude the Great Work revealed in alchemy. The duo particularly aspired to generation of the Philosopher's Stone, the ultimate purpose of spiritual enlightenment.

Aleister Crowley revered Kelly's visions. In *Liber Aleph,* Crowley credits Kelly's visions as the foundation of his Law of Thelema. Crowley also states that he believed Edward Kelly was one of his own previous incarnations. Given Crowley's own reputation as both a rascal and a mystic, the idea has a believable appeal for us today.

– LENURA BARD

pisces

February 19 – March 20

Mutable Sign of Water ▽ Ruled by Neptune ♆

S	M	T	W	T	F	S
				Feb. 19 Nichola Copernicus born, 1473 Capricorn	20 Break a curse	21
22 Aquarius	23 Burn a candle	24 ● Pisces	25 Waxing	26 Keep pebbles in your pocket	27	28 Aries
March 1 Matronalia Taurus	2	3 Correct an error Gemini	4 ◐	5 Search deep for the answer Cancer	6	7 Leo
8 Daylight Savings Time begins at 2 a.m.	9 Read a fairy tale	10 ◯ Chaste Moon Virgo	11 Waning	12 Libra	13 Color eggs	14 Albert Einstein born, 1879 Scorpio
15 Plant vines	16 Sagittarius	17 Laughter banishes fear	18 ◑	19 Minerva's Day Capricorn	20	

Notable Quotations
Prophecy

Every dream is a prophecy.

– George Bernard Shaw

The difference between heresy and prophecy is often one of sequence. Heresy often turns out to have been prophecy – when properly aged.

– Hubert Humphrey

To see clearly is poetry, prophecy and religion – all in one.

– John Ruskin

The best qualification of a prophet is to have a good memory.

– The Marquis of Halifax

If you can look into the seeds of time, and say which grain will grow and which will not, speak then unto me.

– William Shakespeare

She is the Sybil;
  days that distant lie
Bend to the promise that her
  word shall give.

– Thomas Gordon Hake

Prophecy, however honest, is generally a poor substitute for experience.

– Benjamin Cardozo

And it shall come to pass afterward, that I will pour out my spirit upon all flesh; and your sons and your daughters shall prophesy, your old men shall dream dreams, your young men shall see visions.

– Joel 2:28, King James Version

For I dipped into the future,
  far as human eye could see,
Saw the vision of the world, and
  all the wonder that would be.

– Alfred, Lord Tennyson

My interest is in the future because I am going to spend the rest of my life there.

– C.F. Kettering

This is the first age that's ever paid much attention to the future, which is a little ironic since we may not have one.

– Arthur C. Clarke

Window on the Weather

FOR MANY FOLKS, daily weather variations are the greatest concern for planning outdoor activities. A broader understanding of nature's averages may be more helpful for understanding the natural cycles of climate. General trends can make longer-term outdoor plans more realistic, rather than picking out specific weather events. Across the nation, weather conditions will change from year to year, influenced by factors such as El Niño and La Niña and certain solar changes, factors that become apparent shortly before any change of seasons. Longer term, nature's harmony is evident in the stability of longer-term climate averages.

– Tom C. Lang

SPRING

MARCH 2008. The likelihood of heavy snowfall moves north during March. Especially prone are Northern New England, New York State, the Great Plains and Rockies. In fact this is often the snowiest month in the mountainous West, as the jet stream begins its journey north. This is also the beginning of tornado season in the South, with Alabama, Louisiana and North Florida especially vulnerable. Still, balmy temperatures bring pleasant conditions to the Deep South, as coastal locations farther north begin the spring thaw. The West Coast often remains rainy and cool.

APRIL 2008. Even as spring snows remain heavy in western mountains and occasionally in New England, the promise of the season becomes evident elsewhere. The sun brings increasing warmth farther north, to the Carolinas in the East and the desert Southwest. There spring flowers are in full bloom. The tornado risk remains high in the South. Generally these storms, while violent, affect only a small area. Still, their presence should warrant caution. Rainfall can be heavy and winds can gust everywhere. Freezing weather eases from the Ohio Valley to Southern New England. Crops receive abundant moisture in the Plains.

MAY 2008. The frost threat becomes unlikely, with the exception of extreme Northern New England, the Northern Great Lakes and the Northern Rockies. Ocean-born storms ease in the West, while occasional windswept rain can occur in the Northeast. Throughout the Great Plains the weather is generally balmy and sunny with occasional passing thunderstorms. Occasionally the weather can become rough, with passing thunderstorms and isolated tornadoes. The West Coast enjoys brisk Pacific breezes and only a few showers. The Northwest can be foggy.

SUMMER

JUNE 2008. Spring is in full bloom across the entire North. Storms pass along the Canadian border, and here thunderstorms and fast-moving cyclones pass. Sometimes these storms generate hail and a few twisters. East winds still bring Atlantic moisture to the East Coast with some rain and fog occasionally. Sunshine is warmest inland, away from the cool ocean airflow. Annuals are safe to plant everywhere. Lake water temperatures warm in the North. Thunderstorms become daily occurrences on both coasts in Florida.

JULY 2008. On average, the hottest time of the year occurs during the third week of July. This is when the average high temperature, nearly everywhere, is 80 degrees or higher. Ocean water temperatures are also warm enough to reduce the cooling effects of afternoon sea breezes on both the Atlantic and Pacific coasts. Thunderstorms are also prevalent and show up most commonly in Florida, much of the South and along the Continental Divide in the West. Wind flow becomes light and the air becomes more stagnant, with heat and humidity combined bringing the risk for heat exhaustion.

AUGUST 2008. The tropical Atlantic Basin begins to stir in August, with hurricanes first forming in the Caribbean and Gulf of Mexico, and later near the coast of Africa. While the most intense heat of the season eases, temperatures become more moderate in the Far North. In the South, thunderstorms can produce tremendous rainfall and move slowly. The West Coast is dry with fog prevalent in San Francisco and various locations, north and south, along the coast. Cool fronts bring occasional thunderstorms, largely confined to northern states, east of the Rocky Mountains.

AUTUMN

SEPTEMBER 2008. As the hurricane season reaches its peak, September brings great risk of these to the East Coast. An average of one hurricane strike a year occurs from the Gulf States to New England, though the number and intensity of storms can vary. Early frost and a dusting or two of snow can rarely happen in the Northern Rockies. This generally is the driest time of year and the most consistent in temperature variance. Fog is less prevalent near coastal areas, with warm ocean waters dampening onshore airflow.

OCTOBER 2008. October is more than likely the quietest month of weather across the nation. Hurricanes become less frequent, with the threat to coastal areas virtually ending by month's end. Early season frosts are always possible in the valleys of the far north and it is not uncommon to see occasional snowfalls in the Sierra Nevada of California and the Rocky Mountains. With less daylight, mornings turn colder. Leaves turn color by the 15th in much of New England, moving south to the Southern Appalachians by the 31st. Thunderstorms can still be fierce in Florida, though the strongest storms move to the East Coast.

NOVEMBER 2008. This is a month of transition from fall to winter across the North and to a cooler time in the South, where cold fronts pass and north winds follow. The humidity is also lower and outdoor chores more pleasant. November can bring surprising early-season snowfall to New England, though the consistent early winter arrival occurs in the Rockies. Thunderstorms diminish in Florida and become scattered in the Southern Plains. Santa Ana winds bring the threat of fire to Southern California.

WINTER

DECEMBER 2008. Arctic air makes farther intrusions south into the United States. This early in the winter season, the advance is usually short lived, lasting only a few days. The cold air can plunge west of the Continental Divide and affect western states, or plunge east bringing north winds and frigid winds to the Plains, Ohio Valley and New England. Generally, December brings only localized heavy snow, most prevalent near the Great Lakes and occasionally in New England, where early-season coastal storms can form. Pacific-born storms affect the Northwest.

JANUARY 2009. Winter's icy reach is felt fully through much of the country. Winds are strong and combined with midwinter arctic air can plunge wind-chill temperatures below zero across vast reaches of the country. There is also the potential for fast-moving and powdery

snowfalls along the East Coast, as storms generated in the Gulf of Mexico move quickly north. Winter storms can also be strong on the West Coast, where winds can gust past hurricane force from San Francisco to Seattle.

FEBRUARY 2009. Snowfall potential is the greatest across the country during February. Arctic air is firmly entrenched and as the returning sun provides warmth to the South, this temperature contrast can produce intense storms, bringing a foot or more of snow from Washington D.C. to Portland, Maine, with only a few days' notice. The Mid-Continent is generally cold and dry. Depending on the exact position, snowfall can also be very heavy in the mountainous West, preceded by wind-lashed rainfall on the immediate West Coast and its immediate mountain ranges.

Yoruba Divination

Seeking advice from the Otherworld

AMONG THE indigenous faiths of central West Africa, a daily conversation with the ancestors and deities is as commonplace as the dawn of each day. It would be unseemly for a day to begin without a daily prayer of thanks, a libation of cool water and the seeking of advice from the Otherworld.

Central West Africans, particularly the Yoruba, have sought since antiquity to know the nature of the world around them and their own destinies, using a binary-based oracular system known as Ifá. Ifá may be read using kola nuts, sanctified cowrie shells, palm nuts or a "divining chain" made of seed pods. These methods are progressively more complex; the higher versions are read only by initiates and priests.

The term "Ifá" has been identified with the diviner deity Òrúnmìlà, as well as the system of divination. Ifá is the method whereby the word of the high god Olódùmarè and the destiny of the individual are revealed. Reading Ifá is based on the "on" or "off" position of the oracle pieces. Each reflects either the principle of light or the principle of dark. This interplay produces a signature read by the diviner.

The use of the kola nut is the simplest of all methods, used by priests and laity alike. The kola nut has a central position in West African faiths. Many prayers would be considered incomplete without the offering of kola nuts, water and gin.

The kola-nut reading begins during morning prayers, when the elder of the house sanctifies the day. The kola nut is prayed over and then offered to the ancestors or the deity. The nut is touched to a sacred object of the deities/ancestors, then opened. Inside, the kola nut is naturally split into four or more lobes. The supplicant prays for a prosperous day, asking that the offering be accepted. He then takes the lobes of the kola and throws them onto a plate. The convex side (outside) of the kola nut indicates dark and the concave (inside), light. Their combinations reveal one of five signs; here are their brief descriptions:

• *Alafia.* All four lobes face up, indicating all light. This signifies a blessing of peace and health. The offering is accepted.

• *Iwa.* Three lobes up, one lobe down (three light, one dark). This usually indicates that the further questioning is needed to determine if the offering has been accepted.

There are matters of character involved that need to be sorted out.

• *Eji-Ko-Rere/Obi Yan.* Two lobes up and two lobes down (two light, two dark). This is the most propitious of the signs and indicates the offering has unequivocally been accepted. This sign is an indication of perfect balance.

• *Okan.* One lobe up, three lobes down (one light, three dark). There may be difficulty. Further questioning is needed in order to ascertain its nature. Conversely, this can also mean that even though darkness seems to pervade, a light of hope exists.

• *O-Pota-Ku/Isegun.* All four lobes facing down. No light but only darkness. This may seem a bad omen, but in fact many times will indicate a victory over a situation. This sign often indicates that the offering is accepted and that the entity allows for the supplicant to have victory over circumstances. This sign is followed by ritual actions to ensure success.

The next two levels of Ifá are much more complex and are reserved for the various indigenous priesthoods of West African traditions. The cowrie shells, divination chain and palm nuts all involve symbols in a system of sixteen. These tools must be sanctified by many ritual actions before they are used. Their use also takes place within the context of the initiate/priest's consecration to a particular Orisa (deity).

The cowrie shells are considered the mouths of the Orisa, who speaks through the initiate reading them. The sixteen symbols that occur in this system are called *Odu*. Each symbol is associated with a poem that the diviner may recite as the situation demands. These poems illuminate the situation and offer a solution to the questioner. They are sacred in nature and are taken seriously when recited.

The last two methods, the divining chain (also called Opele) and palm nuts (Ikin) are read by the priesthood of the diviner Orisa, Òrún-mìlà. These priest-diviners are known as a *babalawo*, if male, and *iyanifá*, if female (father or mother of secrets). These methods are so identified with this system that they are both referred to simply as Ifá. Both of these methods double the complexity of the cowrie system, raising the number of possible symbols to 256. As with the cowrie divination, poems are recited to illuminate the meaning of the symbols.

The palm nuts are the highest form of Ifá. These objects are given to the *babalawo* or *iyanifá* on their initiation and are used in the priest's worship of Òrúnmìlà. They are very sacred and the process used to read them is painstaking and complex. Understandably, this system is reserved for those truly dedicated to it. Many invocations are done before the reading is generated and the answer is determined. Once given, the answer is considered definitive. The questioner is expected to act on what he or she has been told. These are not systems of fortune telling. They are integral systems generally exercised within a religious/spiritual context. Their messages are held in high regard.

The Yoruba believe that each of us, prior to coming to earth, chose a destiny while kneeling before Olódùmarè. This destiny is embodied in the Òrìsà Orí (personal deity). Our choice becomes intimately entwined with the complex of our inner constellation. We carry this with us in our journey to earth and this, more than anything, is our guiding energy in life. These methods act as a means to discover our forgotten destiny and to guide us towards re-aligning with it. As a system of divination, Ifá shares a common set of symbols with European geomancy, Islamic *ilm al-raml*, Madagascar *sikidy*, Chinese *I-ching* and unnamed systems in India.

Which came first? I would be hard pressed and surely prejudiced in my answer. I believe that these symbols do not know the boundary of language and ethnicity. Perhaps they are all symbols of the meta-language of the Creator. In this respect they relate to all people's mundane concerns of the everyday as well as their seeking esoteric knowledge of destiny.

In your consideration of these matters, may your destiny be bright and may you know and understand it. *Ase*, divine blessings upon you.

– IFADOYIN SANGOMUYIWA
*Nigerian Priest to Sango and
Babalawo, Father of Secrets*

For further details of Ifá divination, visit www.TheWitchesAlmanac.com/almanacextras2008.

Ifadoyin lives in New Jersey, where he also maintains a spiritual house. He can be contacted directly, through his website www.irunmole.org.

Why Wisdom Is Everywhere

A LONG TIME ago, Anansi the spider had all the wisdom in the world stored in a huge pot. Nyame, the sky god, had given it to him. Anansi had been instructed to share it with everyone.

Every day Anansi looked in the pot and learned different things. The pot was full of wonderful ideas and skills. Anansi greedily thought, "I will not share the treasure of knowledge with everyone. I will keep all the wisdom for myself."

So Anansi decided to hide the wisdom on top of a tall tree. He took some vines and made some strong string and tied it firmly around the pot, leaving one end free. He then tied the loose end around his waist so that the pot hung in front of him. He then started to climb the tree. He struggled as he climbed because the pot of wisdom kept getting in his way, bumping against his stomach.

Anansi's son watched in fascination as his father struggled up the tree. Finally Anansi's son told him, "If you tie the pot on your back, it will be easier to cling to the tree and climb." Anansi tied the pot to his back instead, and continued to climb the tree with much more ease.

When Anansi got to the top of the tree, he became angry. "A young one with some common sense knows more than I, and I have the pot of wisdom!"

In anger, Anansi threw down the pot of wisdom. The pot broke and pieces of wisdom flew in every direction. People found the bits scattered everywhere, and if they wanted to they could take some home to their families and friends.

That is why, to this day, no one person has *all* the world's wisdom. People everywhere share small pieces of it whenever they exchange ideas.

– Author unknown
Motherland Nigeria

Decoration from Hausa people, Nigeria

GAMES FOR THE GODDESS

A VERY LONG TIME ago in Greece girls took to running races at religious festivals. Young men liked the idea and they too took to foot racing. From such modest origins over the centuries developed the blockbuster athletic events we still glorify as the Olympics. From the beginning, around the sixth century B.C., the four-day contests were held every four years and were gender distinct. The women's Heraea, dedicated to the goddess Hera, were the first official games held in the vast Olympic Stadium, which could hold 40,000 screaming spectators.

The Heraea Olympics

The Heraea consisted only of foot races run on the men's track, but with a course shortened by one-sixth to correspond with the average shorter stride of women – 192 meters for men, 158 meters for girls. Only maidens, the good old buzzword for virgins, were allowed to compete. They wore tunics that fell just above the knee and bared the right shoulder and breast. Called "chitons," the tunics were ordinarily garments worn by males doing heavy work who needed their right arms free. Why the girls ran in men's clothing is a mystery, compounded by the fact that male Olympic athletes performed nude. Married women were forbidden under pain of death to watch the men's events, deterred by the threat of being hurled off cliffs. The only exception was the priestess of Demeter, a married woman afforded honor seating at an altar of white marble within the stadium

A temple to Zeus dominated the Olympic site, but nearby stood a lovely sanctuary dedicated to Hera, the Ox-Eyed Queen of Heaven. Here before the games girl athletes sacrificed a cow or steer, and winners were awarded the sacred meat. They also won crowns of olive leaves and the right to hang their portraits in the colonnade of the temple. Hera meant everything to the women of ancient Greece. She was the personification of the Great Lady, a powerful divinity in her own right long before her husband/brother Zeus turned up with his thunderbolts. A fertility goddess, Hera blessed weddings, sex within the marriage bed, conception and childbirth. In her later Roman guise as Juno, her name signified the most popular month for weddings.

The first fixed race

According to myth, the games were established by a princess, as beautiful as princesses always are in stories. When Hippodameia came of marriageable age, her father refused to give her in marriage. To discourage suitors, he declared that anyone wishing to marry his daughter must beat him in a chariot race. No one succeeded, for the king sacrificed to Zeus before races and drove horses provided by the god. To further assure success, he decreed that

Hippodameia must ride in the suitor's chariot, adding weight and doubtless distraction.

When the princess saw studly Pelops, she fell wildly in love and determined that he should prevail. First she sacrificed to Hera, pitting the marriage deity's power against Zeus's. Then the clever girl conspired with Myrtilus, her father's driver, to remove the axle pins from the wheels and fill the space with wax. When the wax melted during the course, the wheels flew off and so did the king, who was killed. Hippodameia married her heart's desire, and if there was any regret for a bit of fratricide it has gone unrecorded.

According to the ancient historian Pausanias, "Out of gratitude for her marriage with Pelops, Hippodameia assembled the Sixteen Women, and with them inaugurated the Heraea Games." The Sixteen Women were political activists – rare creatures in a culture where females were seldom seen or heard.

Spartan girls, win intensive

In classical Athens women were relegated to second-class status. They attended to the household, spent long hours at their looms, and seldom left home. The athletes among them were permitted to race, but never encouraged in the same rigorous manner as their brothers. While the boys required training for ten months before entering Olympic events, girls were forbidden to work out. Pericles expressed the male viewpoint of female accomplishment with fiendishly clever irony: "Fame will be great for the woman whose reputation for excellence or blame is least known among males." Nevertheless for women so physically and psychically confined, any chance at running must have provided joyous release for pent-up muscles and minds.

Sparta offered girl athletes a dizzying different world. The military city-state not only encouraged women's sports, but required grueling physical education as institutional policy. In addition to arduous races, girls competed at the javelin and staging battles. They performed nude or in skimpy tunics, the better to attract boys at the events and inspire marriage and procreation. The cultural goal of Sparta was unremittingly eugenic – to develop strong mothers for breeding strong, healthy warriors for the state. Infant girls considered weak were exposed to die. Rather than the regal Hera, Spartan girls identified with the goddess Artemis. Untamed and ferocious, the Divine Huntress roamed the woods with her bow and quiver hunting down animals, the perfect mentor for Spartan girls blazing with a zeal for victory.

Madame Helena Blavatsky

Seeker of divine knowledge

ON August 12, 1831, Helena Petrovna von Hahn was born of distinguished parents in the small Ukrainian town of Ekaterinoslav. Her father was Col. Peter von Hahn, a German officer in Russian service, and her mother was the noted novelist Helena de Fadeyev, daughter of Princess Helena Dolgorukov. Even as a youngster the psychic demonstrated an unusual ability to make deep connections with nature. She adored horses and fearlessly rode the wildest. Helena had also inherited artistic talent from her grandmother, a botanist, and the child excelled at drawing and playing the piano. When she was only eleven years old her mother died. Helena was placed with her maternal grandparents, aristocrats on a feudal estate with never less than fifty serfs.

At the age of seventeen the girl craved independence and decided she had spent enough time under familial authority. She entered into a marriage of convenience with Nikifor V. Blavatsky, a provincial vice-governor more than twice her age. The union was never consummated. Madame Blavatsky fled after three months, but the respectable marital status allowed her to live and travel as she chose.

And travel she did! Helena continued to roam throughout her life, literally spanning the four corners of the globe, and perhaps most significantly long visits to Tibet and India. Mme. Blavatsky met her master, Mahatma Morya or "M", in London when she was twenty. She had envisioned him all her life, she claimed. Blavatsky completely trusted "M", following his guidance in all matters, including her travel itinerary. At the age of twenty-nine HPB began a five-year trek through the Caucasus mountain range, during which time she experienced a physical and psychic breakdown. But at the end of the period Blavatsky emerged in complete control of her psychic gifts and spiritual strength.

Founding the Theosophical Society

When Blavatsky was forty-two, "M" revealed that the thinking world was now ready to receive the wisdom of Theosophia. November 17, 1875, is the official inaugural date of the Theosophical Society. Blavatsky was a principal founder with Colonel Henry Steel Olcott, whom she had met in Vermont, and William Quan Judge, an Irish lawyer. The society set three goals as a mission statement:

- To form a nucleus of the Universal Brotherhood of Humanity, without distinction of race, creed, sex, caste or color.
- To encourage the study of comparative religion, philosophy and science.
- To investigate unexplained laws of nature and the powers latent in man.

The Theosophical Society had a close bond with India. Headquarters were first sited in Bombay and later in Madras before locating to permanent London quarters in 1890.

HPB's life work includes two epic books and two periodicals. In 1877 *Isis Unveiled* was published in New York and the original one thousand copies sold out within ten days. The work compares modern science and theology to their disadvantage against the more esoteric occult sciences and philosophies. The second book, *The Secret Doctrine,* came out in 1888 and is considered the primary major

work. According to Blavatsky herself, it is "the accumulated Wisdom of the Ages." Between the book printings, two magazines emerged from the Theosophical Society. Publication of "The Theosophist" was received as well in India as the author's first book and the number of practitioners multiplied. The second magazine, "Lucifer," was published in London.

And it was in London that Blavatsky died at the age of sixty. Her life was vastly adventurous, both physically and psychically. According to author Theodore Roszak, "Helena Petrovna Blavatsky is surely among the most original and perceptive minds of her time... At the same historical moment that Freud, Pavlov and James had begun to formulate the secularized and materialist theory of mind that has so far dominated Western thought, HPB and her fellow Theosophists were rescuing from occult tradition and exotic religion a forgotten psychology of the superconscious and the extrasensory. Madame Blavatsky may be credited with having set the style for modern occult literature."

– LAURA CONLEY

The Seal of the Theosophical Society

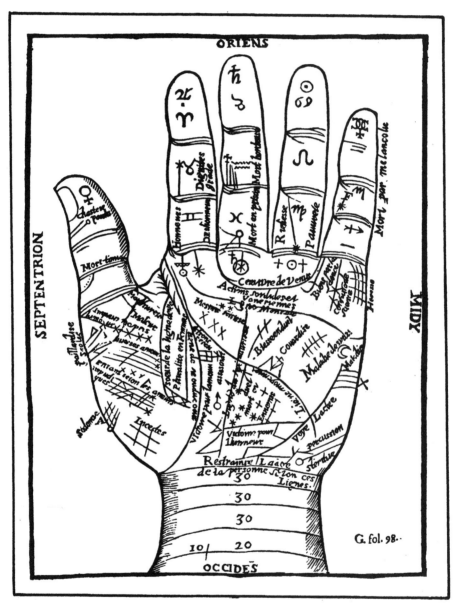

Planetary and zodiacal diagram of the left hand from
Jean Belot's Oeuvres Diverses, *Lyons, 1649*

The Divine Circle
A structure for the seer

CASTING STONES, bones, dice, runes, laying out cards are just a few of the diverse divination methods. Whatever your choice, the process involves a clear question, a symbol system, and a precise design in which the symbols are placed. Trained intuition comes into play for accurate reading and synchronicity too plays a part in the diviner's art.

The choice of a pattern depends on the nature of a question. This pattern is sacred space, where the voice of greater truth may be heard. Regarded as such, divination should be approached with an attitude of respect and attention.

Many layouts can be found in books, while others are transmitted orally as part of a spiritual tradition. A circular pattern, for example, can be found in many traditions and represents the whole or totality of an event for the questioner. In the Tarot, the Wheel of Fortune and the Universe represent this concept, while in astrology the system of Houses signifies the same idea.

In the witch's craft, the eightfold Wheel of the Sabbats is a storehouse of wisdom and experience that speaks to the heart in a familiar language. Such a pattern is potent for divination. You might read using this structure in the following way:

• The center of the wheel signifies the querent or the question.

• To influence the future. Place your symbols of divination (cards, runes, etc.) on the spokes of the wheel to spell out your inner vision. You could use the progression of the Sabbats to bring what you desire closer to you, stage by stage.

• To read for six months prior and six months after a question. Position the Wheel so that the Sabbat closest to the present is towards you, say Beltane, for example. Starting and ending with the opposite Sabbat, Samhain in this instance, cast your symbols clockwise.

• To interpret the forces at play. Each festival represents an area of one's life. Samhain might be Fate; Beltane, choices; Candlemas, home; Lammas, travel. Fall equinox evokes the past, spring, the future. Yule speaks of the seed sleeping in the earth and Midsummer of harmony in nature. Your own and the querent's experiences of these Sabbats also will suggest other meanings.

• To decipher the cause and pattern of an event. Spread clockwise from Samhain, which represents the soil (environment). Yule is the seed, Candlemas the root that grows from it (how it is anchored). Spring shows the stem (the pattern of growing), Beltane resolves into buds (what may be). Midsummer grows into leaf (unfolding), Lammas into flower (emergence). Harvest will be the fruit (the result).

Not only is the eightfold path a wheel of time, space and life, it is a dance to the heartbeat of an ancient harmony. Practice in reading with this pattern will reveal the ancient mysteries to the seer.

– L. Gwalchtan

Messages from Tea

The cup that seers

TEA-LEAF READING has long been recognized as one of the easiest, most popular and comfortable forms of divination. Random signs revealed in the course of daily life have been interpreted through the ages as portents of the future. Intuition is always aided by the release of stress, maintenance of faith, and a sense of goodwill. The warmth of communication and relaxation over a cup of tea offers an atmosphere conducive to psychic perception.

 Use a cup with a rounded bowl. For tea-leaf reading, any loose black tea will do. More rarely, some people also use coffee grounds for divination. Once the cup is prepared, drink the tea to enhance your own essence and intentions. Leave about a half teaspoon of liquid along with some leaves in the bottom of the cup. Concentrate either on a specific question or on the future in general.

Swirl the brew three times clockwise, then tip the cup over on a saucer. Lift and examine the patterns that appear in the cup. Rotate it three times. The immediate future is described by the area at the top of the cup near the handle, the bottom of the cup refers to more distant events. A cup reading is a short-term divination tool; it covers no more than one year. The leaves reveal possibilities and probabilities, but what happens depends upon the individual's decisions made in response to what life offers. Remember that there is always free will.

Watch for patterns that suggest symbols, and then heed your intuition. An anchor, for instance, suggests stable love; a crown, honors, good reputation. Watch for numbers and initials, which can reveal people, places and the timing of important events.

– GRANIA LING

For further details of Tea divination, visit www.TheWitchesAlmanac.com/ almanacextras2008.

DR. MASARU EMOTO

Through water, the power of thought

SEVENTY PERCENT of our planet's surface is water; water constitutes a similar percentage of our very bodies. Water is powerful enough to erode rock, yet bring the most delicate blossoms to life. Humans can live for weeks without food, but only a few days without water. It is one of the basic elements of which the world is made. Throughout the ages, people have honored the essential part water plays in our lives and is honored everywhere by spiritual traditions as a purifier and life giver.

One man wondered if perhaps there isn't even more to learn about water.

Dr. Masaru Emoto has studied the subject for many years through a number of experiments. He is familiar with principles of homeopathy and studies that demonstrate how a mixture of a medicinal compound and water, diluted to the point that the original compound is not detectable, produce the same effects on patients as the undiluted compound. Dr. Emoto wondered if there was some way to demonstrate physical evidence that water somehow "memorized" the information conveyed by the original compound. At another time he remembered that "no two snow crystals are exactly the same," which led him to freeze water and examine the crystals.

After perfecting a technique to create and photograph water crystals, Dr. Emoto looked at the water around him. He started with tap water in Tokyo and water collected directly from the rivers and springs. The crystals from the city were incomplete; those found in nature were complete and beautiful. Dr. Emoto tried experiments wherein water was exposed to different kinds of music. Classical music created well-formed crystals; crystals influenced by heavy metal music were fragmented and malformed. Proceeding further, bottles of water were provided with different labels having the words facing into the bottles. "Thank you" water formed perfect hexagonal crystals; "you fool" crystals looked like those exposed to heavy metal music. Dr. Emoto's experiments consistently demonstrated that not only did water crystals change when exposed to different influences, but that the shapes of the crystals reflected the positive or negative aspects of the chosen influence. Somehow the water understood and reflected what was around it.

But how? Dr. Emoto postulated that vibrations emanated from the influences to which the water was exposed and that those vibrations changed the water. He called the vibrations "hado" and assumed that hado energy existed throughout the universe. Using a machine to measure those vibrations, he developed hado medicine. Just as overlaying one sound wave with its opposite cancels the original sound, Dr. Emoto found he could ease a patient's suffering by having her drink water "programmed" with vibrations opposite those emitted by the patient.

Dr. Emoto measured the hado present in assorted foods and found those we consider healthiest – vegetables, lean meats – to be the highest in hado. Further, he found that food prepared with loving words measured even higher, while foods treated in a microwave were lower. This led to experiments exposing water to assorted technologies such as computers, TVs, and cell phones, all of which failed to produce well-formed crystals. When that same water was labeled with loving words, the ill effects of the hi-tech devices were reversed. The most healing words? "Love and gratitude."

Dr. Emoto demonstrated the healing effects of directed thought on several lakes throughout the world. In Japan, Brazil, and Germany, lake water that produced plain or even malformed crystals was prayed over. In all three places, crystals examined after the prayer were well-formed and complex.

It's no secret that we are affected by the world around us and the daily stresses to which we are subjected. My moods are affected by the movies I watch, the music I listen to, the words I hear. It seems to me that I am processing all of these inputs in my computer brain, associating them with past events and influences, and feeling certain emotions as a result. Is it possible that the change is attributable to the simple mechanism of vibrations?

Quantum physics and the Principle of Uncertainty demonstrate that light is neither a particle nor a wave but some combination of the two, the manifestation of which depends on how it is observed. Dr. Emoto tells a story of a family giving negative attention to one jar of rice and positive attention to another. After a month, the negative rice turned black; the positive rice fermented and smelled of malt. In another experiment a third jar was ignored. That jar rotted even faster than the jar given negative attention. Observation necessarily changes the thing that is observed. Observation (attention) equals energy; positive attention yields positive (qualitative) change. What is it that travels invisibly through space to affect the change? Physics suggests that energy vibrations rather than material particles are the fundamental "stuff" of our reality.

Dr. Emoto is not the only person who believes that everything is made of or contains energy. Some people call it "chi," some call it "mana," some even call it "the Force." Many people testify to the powers of prayer and positive thinking. Skilled meditators produce states in their own bodies that science cannot explain. Studies of the brain have shown that positive thoughts physically change the workings of the brain that does the thinking. Is it possible that we truly are created in the Maker's image – with the power of the creation of our very realities at our disposal on a literal level?

Dr. Emoto states that "consciousness creates all." Is water the mechanism of the changes Dr. Emoto demonstrated or is it simply another example of the change that consciousness can affect? Did heavy metal music destroy the crystals in the water or did Dr. Emoto's expectations? Far more sophisticated experiments with much stricter controls are required to tease apart all the factors at work in such situations.

Whether you believe in Dr. Emoto's hado-measuring machine or not, it is apparent that something very real is happening. Perhaps water really does reflect the energy directed towards it the same way that it mirrors the surrounding landscape. Perhaps the water in Dr. Emoto's experiments was reflecting not the stimuli presented, but the doctor's own expectations. Whatever the cause of the change, there is no denying that some change took place.

It is one thing to know in a metaphorical sense that I am in control of my happiness, that I am responsible for my choices and have the power to decide what will and will not be allowed in my life. It is quite another to see change literally in front of my eyes. Dr. Emoto's research provides one more piece of compelling evidence that loving thoughts and kind words have power. Whether that power is in the water that sustains us or a nexus of energy vibrations of which we are part, it is humbling to imagine what could be accomplished if our consciousness were directed toward love and peace for all.

– Brigid and Willow

Dikki-Jo Mullen, our staff astrologer, is similarly fascinated with Dr. Masaru Emoto. She has provided us with his astrological chart and an account of a Florida lecture she enjoyed. See page 72.

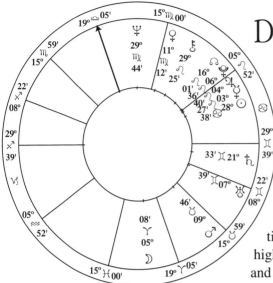

Dr. Masaru Emoto
An astrological view

DR. EMOTO IS touring the world presenting a new hope for peace, health and longevity on the planet through developing a positive relationship with water. While Dr. Emoto was in the U.S., I was fortunate enough to attend a lecture offered by him when he presented his water research at the Unity Church in Melbourne, Florida.

I explained my work and asked the doctor if he would be kind enough to provide his birth data. With a gracious bow he gave me the information. Dr. Emoto was born on July 22, 1943, just before 5 p.m., in Yokohama. Of course he is a water sign. His Sun is in home- and family-oriented Cancer in the 7th house. During the program he referred often to his beloved wife, children and grandchildren. Emoto joked, saying that he wasn't a typical Japanese in that he freely praised and bragged about his family. His message reaches out to children, especially encouraging those from three to twelve years of age to connect with water in a spiritual and peaceful way. His Sun is sextile Neptune, which is in the 9th house in Virgo. This is a very sensitive, creative and mystical aspect. The 9th house accents higher education, foreign languages and travel. Dr. Emoto's work has been translated into many languages and his publications are available the world over. Venus is also in Virgo. This shows an appreciation for health and purity as well as precision. Venus is trine Mars in Taurus in the 4th house. Taurus always has a strong link to the Earth. Ecology and a respect for the Earth as our home are emphasized strongly in Dr. Emoto's work. Recently he introduced Al Gore's epic work, *An Inconvenient Truth*, to audiences in Japan, where it has become an instant hit.

Masaru Emoto is quite a showman. A clever speaker, he used humor as well as audio visual aids during his presentation. His books are lavishly illustrated. He has a stellium in flamboyant Leo, the actor's sign. This includes a Mercury-Jupiter-Pluto conjunction as well as the North Node and Chiron. The Leo planets span most of the sign and impact both the 7th and 8th houses.. This promises pride, quality, an affinity with the very young and research ability. His Moon is in Aries in the 3rd house. This brings the spirit of the pioneer to the fore and also allows him to put his emotions into his words. The 3rd house represents basic education, versatility and information exchange. Emoto's products include a variety of teaching tools. He has published books, CD's, water crystal oracle cards, bumper stickers, greeting cards and created a hexagonal-charged drinking water, and more. Saturn and Uranus are in Gemini. This again reveals communication skill and versatility. Saturn is in the 6th house. This house ties in with health care, service and animals.

Some of Emoto's most striking water pictures were programmed with the names of animals. Dolphins and elephants appeared in the water crystals programmed with their names. A more solemn message was also shown during the presentation. An aerial photograph of the destructive tsunami revealed a perfectly formed dragon image coiling along the beach ahead of the killer wave. Emoto noted that in Japan, the spirit of water is portrayed as an animal in the form of a dragon. Uranus is on the cusp of the 5th and 6th houses. This combines innovations in health care as well as creativity involving children.

The time of birth that Dr. Emoto gave places his ascendant (rising sign) on the last degree of the fire sign of Sagittarius. This shows his sincerity as well as giving him the aura of a prophet and teacher. He has a rare talent for crossing cultural barriers to touch the hearts and minds of many types of people all around the world.

Dr. Emoto was born with no retrograde planets. This indicates that he is a very progressive individual who can leave behind old barriers and concepts. He is truly an architect of the future. With more planets above the horizon (in houses 7 through 12) than below, he tends to be expressive and an extrovert. He has many more planets in the western half of the birth map (houses 4 through 9) than in the East. This shows that external circumstances can guide the course of his life. His free will is impacted by others. His Moon was in the disseminating phase and waning at birth. This reveals that he is a natural teacher. Dr. Emoto will always be inspired to share the wisdom and life experiences he has gained in order to uplift others.

– DIKKI-JO MULLEN

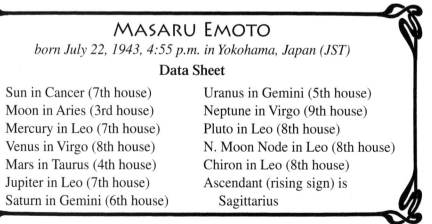

MASARU EMOTO

born July 22, 1943, 4:55 p.m. in Yokohama, Japan (JST)

Data Sheet

Sun in Cancer (7th house)	Uranus in Gemini (5th house)
Moon in Aries (3rd house)	Neptune in Virgo (9th house)
Mercury in Leo (7th house)	Pluto in Leo (8th house)
Venus in Virgo (8th house)	N. Moon Node in Leo (8th house)
Mars in Taurus (4th house)	Chiron in Leo (8th house)
Jupiter in Leo (7th house)	Ascendant (rising sign) is
Saturn in Gemini (6th house)	Sagittarius

Algenubi

Wisdom from the Lion's mouth

FIXED STARS, along with the mansions of the Moon and constellations, are part of astrology's most ancient heritage. Centuries before zodiac signs, aspects or houses were ever used, the dedicated astrologers of Egypt, India, China and Central America interpreted and analyzed the stars. Their observations were then related to the earthly experiences of human beings through the universally respected doctrine "as above, so below."

During the past twenty years, modern astrologers have gained access to updated star lists with the help of new technology. This aspect of astrology, once guarded carefully by the most learned of scholars, can now benefit all who would explore the wisdom of the heavens in greater depth and detail. As Manilius, a great Roman astrologer, wrote in his book *Astronomica* (c. 10 A.D.), "You must not divert attention from the smallest detail; nothing exists without reason or has been uselessly created." The universe is within and a part of us, nothing is coincidental or accidental.

The many stars twinkling in the sky are individual Suns. Each one radiates its unique energy field. This cosmic power impacts us always. The brightness of the stars, called the magnitude, as well as the temperature, as revealed by the color, provide clues as to the exact nature of the stellar energy being sent. The vistas of space separating the stars from each other and from Earth are so vast that we can barely conceive of it. To facilitate comprehension, a unit of measurement called a light year was developed. This is the distance that light, which moves at 186,330 miles each second, travels in a year's time. The closest stars are at least four light years away. The term "fixed star" is actually a misnomer. The stars do move, but so slowly that a change in position is barely perceptible over the span of a century. When the Sun, Moon or a planet conjoins or is parallel a fixed star, the nature of the star will have a profound impact. Other aspects, such as a trine or opposition, are said to "cast no rays" regarding fixed stars; that is, they have no influence.

A conjunction with a fixed star to placements in the horoscope at birth is of lifelong importance. If the star's influence is a passing one, a transit, then the symbols and keynotes of the star will have an important impact for a given period of time.

On February 9, 2009 at 9:49 a.m., Eastern Standard Time, there will be a partial eclipse of the Full Moon at 21 degrees Leo 0 minutes. The fixed star Algenubi , which is at 20 degrees Leo 42 minutes, will be in a close conjunction to the eclipse point. During the weeks following the eclipse, this star will have universal influence. A Full Moon celebration altar dedicated to Lions would be an appropriate way to honor the brightest and best side of Algenubi.

Algenubi is an abbreviation for the Arabic, *Ras Elased Aust,* meaning "he who rends." The Strength Card, Key VIII in the Major Arcana of the Tarot, is closely related to this star. Algenubi is a yellow star of the 3rd magnitude located in the Lion's mouth area in the constellation Leo. It is ninety-five light years away from Earth. Algenubi's nature is neutral, meaning that how it is used depends upon choice and circumstances. The eternal struggle between good and evil is embodied in Algenubi, which has a Mars-Saturn nature. Creative, artistically appreciative, theatrical, flamboyant and expressive yet potentially pretentious are keynotes of this star. Extremes of both cruelty and kindness are present.

All of those born from August 11-15 of any year have Algenubi conjunct the Sun at birth. In other horoscopes, planets within a two-degree orb of the twenty-first degree of Leo are likewise permanently blended with Algenubi. The wise will heed the messages sent by this influential and mighty star.

Lights shining in the void
Stars symbolize the spirit
Of the divine struggle
To overcome the deepest darkness.

– Dikki-Jo Mullen

Moon Cycles

A New Moon rises with the Sun,
Her waxing half at midday shows,
The Full Moon climbs at sunset hour,
And waning half the midnight knows.

NEW	2009	FULL	NEW	2010	FULL
January 26		January 10	January 15		January 30
February 24		February 9	February 13		February 28
March 26		March 10	March 15		March 29
April 24		April 9	April 14		April 28
May 24		May 9	May 13		May 27
June 22		June 7	June 12		June 26
July 21		July 7	July 11		July 25
August 20		August 5	August 9		August 24
September 18		September 4	September 8		September 23
October 18		October 4	October 7		October 22
November 16		November 2	November 6		November 21
December 16		December 2/31	December 5		December 21

Life takes on added dimension when you
match your activities to the waxing and waning of the Moon.
Observe the sequence of her phases to learn
the wisdom of constant change within complete certainty.

presage

by Dikki-Jo Mullen

ARIES 2008 — PISCES 2009

Always, the stars promise, there is a way. Solutions to life's dilemmas usually come about after taking a break and backing away to gain perspective. The year ahead is a cycle for new beginnings. Prepare to soar.

Since the time of Pythagoras, the wisdom of numerology and astrology have been linked. 2008 is a One Year in numerology (2 + 0 + 0 + 8 = 10 and 1 + 0 = 1). During a One Year the choices made determine the foundation which directs the next nine years. A mood of birth, youth, and springtime prevails. Start over, take a new approach. Innovate and invent.

The Chinese calendar also brings news of changing times and fresh directions. This is the Year of the Rat. The first of the animal signs arrives to greet a whole new cycle. Various ancient prophecies which advise that the familiar world and traditional values are to undergo a metamorphosis are coming true daily. Astrology is a wonderful tool to help make your journey into the future a joyful and rewarding one. After reading your familiar birth sign, called the Sun sign, consult the sections related to your Moon and ascendant or rising sign for deeper insight.

This year's eclipses, two each in Leo and Aquarius, will impact leisure and recreation as well as advances in technology, politics, and humanitarian organizations. Look for surprises and upsets in the status quo involving these areas. With serious Saturn in health-conscious Virgo, concerns about medical care, diet, and nutrition can be a focus. With Jupiter and Pluto in Capricorn, new ways to use the resources of our planet, ecology, and the economy are also likely to be of significance.

ASTROLOGICAL KEYS

Signs of the Zodiac
Channels of Expression

ARIES: fiery, pioneering, competitive
TAURUS: earthy, stable, practical
GEMINI: dual, lively, versatile
CANCER: protective, traditional
LEO: dramatic, flamboyant, warm
VIRGO: conscientious, analytical
LIBRA: refined, fair, sociable
SCORPIO: intense, secretive, ambitious
SAGITTARIUS: friendly, expansive
CAPRICORN: cautious, materialistic
AQUARIUS: inquisitive, unpredictable
PISCES: responsive, dependent, fanciful

Elements

FIRE: Aries, Leo, Sagittarius
EARTH: Taurus, Virgo, Capricorn
AIR: Gemini, Libra, Aquarius
WATER: Cancer, Scorpio, Pisces

Qualities

CARDINAL	FIXED	MUTABLE
Aries	Taurus	Gemini
Cancer	Leo	Virgo
Libra	Scorpio	Sagittarius
Capricorn	Aquarius	Pisces

CARDINAL signs mark the beginning of each new season — active.
FIXED signs represent the season at its height — steadfast.
MUTABLE signs herald a change of season — variable.

Celestial Bodies
Generating Energy of the Cosmos

Sun: birth sign, ego, identity
Moon: emotions, memories, personality
Mercury: communication, intellect, skills
Venus: love, pleasures, the fine arts
Mars: energy, challenges, sports
Jupiter: expansion, religion, happiness
Saturn: responsibility, maturity, realities
Uranus: originality, science, progress
Neptune: dreams, illusions, inspiration
Pluto: rebirth, renewal, resources

Glossary of Aspects

Conjunction: two planets within the same sign or less than 10 degrees apart, favorable or unfavorable according to the nature of the planets.

Sextile: a pleasant, harmonious aspect occurring when two planets are two signs or 60 degrees apart.

Square: a major negative effect resulting when planets are three signs from one another or 90 degrees apart.

Trine: planets four signs or 120 degrees apart, forming a positive and favorable influence.

Quincunx: a mildly negative aspect produced when planets are five signs or 150 degrees apart.

Opposition: a six sign or 180 degrees separation of planets generating positive or negative forces depending on the planets involved.

The Houses — *Twelve Areas of Life*

1st house: appearance, image, identity
2nd house: money, possessions, tools
3rd house: communications, siblings
4th house: family, domesticity, security
5th house: romance, creativity, children
6th house: daily routine, service, health
7th house: marriage, partnerships, union
8th house: passion, death, rebirth, soul
9th house: travel, philosophy, education
10th house: fame, achievement, mastery
11th house: goals, friends, high hopes
12th house: sacrifice, solitude, privacy

ECLIPSES

From very first astrological records, eclipses have been linked to surprise and transformation. The most influential eclipses involve the Sun or Moon and feature an exact alignment with the Earth. The keyword for an eclipse is "change."

Take note if the degree of an eclipse is within three degrees of a planet in your birth chart. It will amplify the inherent promise of that planet. An eclipse within three days of the birthday augurs an interesting year and can mean a move, job change, or new cycle in your personal life. Don't force issues during an eclipse. Instead observe, then respond. The year ahead brings four eclipses.

August 1, 2008	New Moon Solar in Leo, south node – total
August 16, 2008	Full Moon Lunar in Aquarius, north node – partial
January 26, 2009	New Moon Solar in Aquarius, north node – partial
February 9, 2009	Full Moon Lunar in Leo, north node – partial

PLANETS IN RETROGRADE MOTION

Retake, re-evaluate, retrace, and revamp during a retrograde cycle to make it a beneficial time. Although a retrograde is an optical illusion created by the planet's speed of travel relative to the Earth's rate of motion, its impact is very significant. It promises a shift in established situations. There can be a chance to overcome a mistake or to reverse a disappointment. The past resurfaces to influence the present. All that is ruled by the retrograde planet will be most impacted.

Mercury Retrograde Cycles
Three or four times yearly, for about three weeks, retrograde Mercury delays travel, scrambles appointments, and brings back people from the past. The wise witch will tread familiar paths and complete old projects. Changes made during a Mercury retrograde can lack permanence and be unstable. Use caution about making a promise or signing a contract. Retrograde Mercury cycles favor past life regression, reunions, and visiting places of historical interest. Geminis and Virgos feel Mercury retrograde most keenly.

May 26 – June 19, 2008
in Gemini

September 24 – October 15, 2008
in Libra

January 11 – February 1, 2009
in Aquarius and Capricorn

Venus Retrograde Cycle
Venus turns retrograde on March 6, 2009 in Aries where it remains through the winter's end. Taurus and Libra people notice this retrograde especially. Use caution in changing the status of intimate relationships. Be tolerant of those who seem impolite or who have different tastes. Venus retrograde affects matters of the heart, social graces, and the fine arts.

ARIES

The year ahead for those
born under the sign of the Ram
March 20–April 19

Enterprising and confident, Rams are born with the springtime and ruled by dynamic Mars. Excitable and rather impatient, you are drawn to new and novel ventures. That which drags on or is repetitious will soon be abandoned. Schedule appointments and begin projects on Tuesdays, your lucky day. Events tend to turn in your favor when pursued on that day.

Spring's first days find you working hard to comfort family members. Changes concerning your residence and needed repairs are likely. Mars is creating a stir in your 4th house. On April 7 Venus enters your sign where it remains until May Eve. Your charm and beauty impress the right people and help is offered. Pursue social opportunities. Artistic aptitudes are heightened. From early May until mid-July Mercury remains in your 3rd house in a sextile aspect to the Sun, bringing tremendous mental energy. New ideas abound. Short journeys will be refreshing. A neighbor is helpful and has knowledge to share.

As Midsummer's Day nears Mars trines your Sun. This influence provides the extra motivation you need to excel by the end of June. Early July finds cardinal sign planets, including Jupiter, pulling you in different directions. Seek balance. Near the Full Moon on July 18, compromise is a must. The remainder of the month finds Venus in your love and pleasure sector. There is time to relax with a dear one or pursue a favorite pastime. The eclipses on August 1 and 16 usher in new goals and priorities. Accept changes in your social circle philosophically. Those near you are growing, and with growth comes change.

The first autumn breezes bring an appreciation for the best use of time. Establish an efficient schedule. Saturn in Virgo is activated by other earth sign transits in September, generating a practical, earthy attitude. Find a corner for a circle of crystals or a potted herb to invite the aid of friendly earth elementals into your work space. The Aries Full Moon of October 14 forms a cardinal t-square. This ushers in an interesting, but hectic month. Double-check instructions and directions. A difficult Mercury opposition hints at some impending mix-ups. Ask questions and verify. Be patient if a piece of work has to be redone.

From All Hallows Eve through mid-November, Venus brightens your 9th house. Ritual work incorporating music and art from faraway lands can elevate your spirit. Grandparent and grandchild interactions will be especially happy and comforting. From November 17 through Yuletide Mars moves through your sister fire sign of Sagittarius. Outdoor fire ceremonies can evoke a new sense of the sacred. This is also a wonderful time for a spiritual pilgrimage. While walking or engaging in other active pursuits you can sense a deeper connection with your higher self. In early January Jupiter joins Mercury and Neptune in your 11th house. Community involvement will be rewarding. A mission to make the world a better place has appeal. You'll enjoy a renewed appreciation for cherished friendships too. As Candlemas nears, Mars influences your career sector. Competitors provide inspiration, but professional obligations can be stressful. Take time to relax and regroup if you start to feel pressured.

Venus enters Aries to conjoin your Sun at the beginning of February. This benevolent transit remains through winter's end. The Full Moon eclipse on February 9 is a wonderful time to explore which way your heart really leans. A revelation about the meaning of true love, for either a person or an important interest, can be realized near Valentine's Day. The remainder of February will be very upbeat; both love and finances are promising. During March, Mercury and the Sun join Uranus in your 12th house. Take note of your dreams; a meaningful message might be encoded in the symbols. You'll enjoy times of quiet reverie as winter wanes. There are thoughts and feelings you might prefer to keep to yourself for the time being.

HEALTH
Serious Saturn remains in Virgo, your 6th house of health, all year. It's a time when you will reap what has been sown. This suggests that natural whole grains would be good for you. You're aware of the affects of past health-related decisions. A favorable Jupiter aspect promises that healing and enhanced fitness will be the reward of the efforts you make to develop good health habits. As for making any change, patience is important.

LOVE
Eclipses on August 1 and February 9 occur in your 5th house of love. This promises surprise and change regarding tender passions. A current relationship could either phase out or intensify. A sudden attraction can shine the light of love on those Aries natives who have been lonely. Venus turns retrograde in your birth sign in March 2009. This suggests a reunion with someone from the past. However, the last weeks of winter are not favorable for finalizing either a commitment or a breakup. Preserve the status quo. Wait and watch before making any giant leaps.

SPIRITUALITY
Pluto completes a transit which began in 1995 in your 9th house of spirituality. You have gone through deep transformations since then in your most fundamental beliefs. Now is a time when you will integrate what you've learned. By the end of November a deep realization of what faith and truth really mean in your life will crystallize.

FINANCE
Favorable aspects from both Jupiter and Saturn to the cusp of your 2nd house of finance indicate financial gains during the year to come. However, your overhead could be high, especially during July and October. Meditate on ways to cut back on expenses. Resale shops or bargain bins can hold some pleasant surprises.

TAURUS

*The year ahead for those
born under the sign of the Bull*
April 20 – May 20

The Bull, your emblem, has long represented wealth. Quality and security are always top priorities. There's a sensual side present, and you definitely have a taste for life's finer things. Ruled by Venus, you are affectionate and appreciate the arts, especially music. Friday is your lucky day each week. Make purchases and decisions then to enhance success.

Early spring brings the gift of friendship. From the vernal equinox until April 6, a favorable Venus influence brightens your 11th house. Get involved with groups, cultivate those whom you would enjoy as friends. Politics and community issues can be a catalyst for association. As May Eve nears, Mercury moves rapidly through your sign. Travel is educational and profitable. It's an excellent time to purchase books or enroll in study programs. Throughout May, Venus forms a grand trine aspect in Earth signs with Saturn in Virgo and Jupiter and Pluto in Capricorn. This marks one of the most promising times all year. Career and personal opportunities abound. Enjoy life and put plans in motion for future dreams. Honor Mother Earth with fresh flowers in your meditation area. Plant a garden or grow kitchen herbs on a windowsill.

Early June finds retrograde Mercury in your 2nd house. Watch habits regarding spending and cash flow. Conversations revolve around business. Devote the summer solstice to prosperity magic. A talisman of gold and jade blessed by the light of an emerald candle would be helpful. Home decorating, improvements, and entertaining are on your agenda during July when Leo transits affect your 4th house. By Lammas a new love and appreciation for family and home life develops. Prepare a keepsake scrapbook honoring summer vacation memories. Mars, Mercury, and Venus form a stellium in your health sector during September. Written affirmations can be very helpful regarding health goals. Also make daily working conditions as wholesome and peaceful as possible. At Mabon purchase or make a gift for a special animal companion. A deepening bond of love and respect will be forged with the creature. The gift might be a fresh catnip sachet for a favored feline, a feeder for wild winged ones, or a colorful new bandana tied around the neck of a loyal canine.

By mid-October the influence of Mercury retrograde in your 6th house creates some chaos in daily routine. Get organized and double-check details. Strong Mars aspects near Samhain will encourage you to splurge or take a gamble. Do enjoy some special goodies or luxuries in moderation, but don't go to extremes. The Taurus Full Moon of November 13 is supported by benevolent Venus-Jupiter influences. You'll realize that there is so much to appreciate and be thankful for by the month's end. December begins with a planetary alignment in your 8th house of mysteries. In the dark, magical days before Yuletide, a puzzle is solved. Expect contact with the spirit world. The presence of those who have passed on lingers, offering solace and wisdom during your meditations.

Your energy level is high as January begins. Mars in your sister earth sign of Capricorn conjoins both Jupiter and Pluto to foster your overall vitality and enthusiasm. Write your New Year's resolutions, schedule appointments, and begin projects you've been interested in. Through Candlemas you can set great things in motion. The eclipse of February 9 brings a surprise regarding home and family life. Prepare for a change, maybe involving a move before winter ends. By late February Jupiter, Mars, and Mercury all join Neptune in Aquarius. This powerful pattern clusters in your sector of recognition and career. Be alert to changes in your field. Very keen competition is present. Dispel confusion by double-checking for precision and accuracy. Be diplomatic during discussions. An uncharitable comment made would come back to haunt you. March finds Venus turning retrograde in your 12th house. Memories of a lost love must be kept in perspective. Your interest in helping the disadvantaged or in addressing ecological concerns grows. Quietly, you will act and do much good in the world. This is especially true near the Full Moon in Virgo on March 10.

HEALTH

Because you have partnership-oriented Libra ruling your health sector, emotional well-being is always a contributing factor to your level of physical wellness. In other words, if someone you care about is ill, you're affected. If a relationship goes awry, you can become unwell. Be aware of how others affect your health and make an effort to detach a bit. The lower back and kidney regions can be the source of health concerns this year, especially during the autumn. Drink plenty of cranberry juice and water. Consider scheduling a chiropractic adjustment.

LOVE

Sober Saturn is favorably positioned in your 5th house of romance all year. Commitments stabilize. Be receptive to an involvement with an attractive person who is of a different generation. Working with those you are attracted to can also lead to personal intimacy. A love-related goal is accomplished during August.

SPIRITUALITY

Plan a pilgrimage to an area with mountainous terrain. Meditate, connect with the earth forces. Jupiter in Capricorn remains in your 9th house from springtime through the winter solstice. This promises an expansion in consciousness. Participation in a traditional Native American medicine wheel ceremony could offer profound spiritual awakening.

FINANCE

From late May through the summer solstice a retrograde Mercury in your financial sector brings opportunities to correct old financial problems or fulfill financial obligations. Pluto crossing into Capricorn this year hints at profits coming to you from inheritance, investments, or past work. Pursue promising new opportunities in May, August, and December.

GEMINI

*The year ahead for those
born under the sign of the Twins*
May 21 – June 20

Inquisitive and intellectual Mercury is your planet. The Twins symbolize information exchange and duality. Gemini is always at least two people in one and will adapt to surroundings and circumstances. Make choices and pursue goals on Wednesdays, your lucky day each week.

Career prospects are both interesting and challenging as spring begins. Venus and Uranus stroll through your 10th house together from the vernal equinox through early April. Innovate, be creative. Combine business with pleasure. Listen carefully to others during the last three weeks of April. Several transits in your sector of friendship indicate that valuable information is offered during social situations and at meetings. Just after Beltane, Mercury begins a very long transit through Gemini which lasts until mid-July. Your natural quickness and cleverness are enhanced. Travel prospects are very promising. It's a perfect time to begin writing a book, assembling artistic creations, or selecting educational goals. Celebrate your birthday with the purchase of new finery or jewelry. It's a bright and happy time. Venus is close to a conjunction with your Sun.

Shortly after the summer solstice, Mars joins Saturn in your home and family sector. Work out anger issues with relatives. Compromise is the solution to domestic conflicts. Your residence might need some maintenance before the end of July. Devote the Lammastide sabbat to blessings for your home. The August eclipse pattern affects your travel sectors. A new vehicle might be purchased; new methods of transportation can be helpful. Mobility is especially important to your happiness, for your mercurial nature is especially in evidence during late summer. September brings improvements in your love life and vacation prospects. Several planets, including Venus and Mars, cuddle together in your 5th house of pleasure. Reach out to the one you are drawn to. Your feelings are reciprocated. Love magic is especially effective near Mabon.

October's retrograde Mercury accents your health. Observe how health patterns repeat; resolve to form good habits for wellness. You might require extra rest. Relaxation is the best gift you can give yourself through mid-October. Near the Full Moon of October 14 dreams can have added significance. Be sensitive to different viewpoints as Samhain nears. Transits in Sagittarius, your opposing sign, are gathering in your 7th house. Cooperation and tolerance are essential through late October and November. You'll be aware of the importance of upholding justice and maintaining balance. The Full Moon in your sign on December 12 favorably aspects Neptune. A deep spiritual awareness of the Yuletide season's significance is present. Your intuition is wonderful during

December. Heed those inner voices and you'll be guided toward success.

Early January marks the onset of a yearlong Jupiter transit through Aquarius, your sister air sign. This highlights your 9th house, sector of the higher mind. Your aspirations are moving to a higher plane. Prepare for journeys of the mind and body. Some Geminis will enroll in educational programs; others might explore other countries or be drawn to learn more about another religion. All that is foreign and remote will pave the route to good fortune in 2009. The New Moon eclipse on January 26 will reveal the specifics concerning how this will affect you on a personal level.

At Candlemas Mercury goes direct in your 8th house. Financial obligations relating to others can be resolved. Sincerity is the best way to process and release old resentments. Get in tune with how you really feel and letothers know. A positive Mars aspect is in force through March 14. Your vitality is good and you can overcome competition or other obstacles with aplomb. Prepare a ritual using fire and ice to focus the valuable energy you have now in the most beneficial direction. Retrograde Venus at winter's end affects your close friends. Expect news of a status change concerning a couple to whom you're close.

HEALTH

This year Pluto, ruler of your 6th house of health, begins a long-term quincunx aspect to your Sun. The Sun is the energy source of all life, while the quincunx is an aspect of fate and circumstances. Hereditary health factors as well as the influences of the environment can affect your well-being. Cope by being sensitive to your body. Take care of it. Honor it with the best health habits and diet. The body is the temple of the spirit.

LOVE

A trine from mystical Neptune aspects your love sector all year. You're idealistic about love. Air sign influences are prominent. Cultivate a lighthearted approach to relationships. Share jokes and poetry, travel or good books with one whom you would woo. From August 20 – November 4 several planetary transits moving through your 5th house promise opportunities to develop a happy, nurturing relationship.

SPIRITUALITY

The eclipses on August 16 and January 26 impact your 9th house of spirituality. Adorn a ritual altar or meditation area with representations of the spiritual direction you would like to take. Be receptive to new truths, for an eclipse promises changes and discovery. When Jupiter enters your spiritual sector on January 6, a cycle of profound spiritual awakening begins. During 2009 plan at least one journey to a sacred site.

FINANCE

Others might offer advice or funding that will help you financially this year. Jupiter and Pluto both affect your 8th house then. Investments, an inheritance, or a partner's income can supplement your own earnings. The New Moon on July 2 falls in your 2nd house of earned income. This begins a wonderful four-week cycle for evaluation of your salable skills. Explore rewarding new trends in employment during summer's warm, bright days.

CANCER

The year ahead for those
born under the sign of the Crab
June 21 – July 22

Fluctuating like the Moon, Cancer is responsive, emotional, and generous. Moon children have an empathy with others and a wonderful, warm sense of humor. However, there is insecurity to overcome. Like your emblem, the Crab, your exterior shields a soft inner self. Mondays are your luckiest days each week. Commit to activities and make choices on Mondays for best results.

Spring's earliest days favor writing, travel, and philosophical studies. From the vernal equinox through All Fool's Day, Mercury joins Venus and Uranus in your 9th house. Mars remains in your sign through May 9. Much can be accomplished because your energy level will be exceptionally high, but do quell anger and impatience. It's especially easy to overreact near the Full Moon on April 20. Consider consequences and options first. From May 3 through mid-July Mercury highlights your 12th house. Quiet the mind through meditation. Psychic communication with wild creatures will be especially lucid. Just before Midsummer's Eve Venus enters Cancer. Devote the longest day of the year to love magic. Near your birthday your creative talents shine. Use your imagination.

The last half of July finds Mercury flying through Cancer. Impromptu travel would be productive. Your clever repartee enables you to win all arguments. At Lammas, Leo transits align in your financial sector. Prepare a prosperity ritual and bless your workplace. Early August is a wonderful time to explore your financial options. After August 11 Mercury joins Venus and Saturn in your sector of communication. Letters and conversations will be serious, but decisions can be made and helpful advice exchanged. Avoid a difficult neighbor or troubled sibling. Throughout September, Mars impacts home and family life. Patiently work out differences and make needed repairs. Shop for the best prices. A square from Mars to Jupiter can lead to extravagance or overpayment. A relative is feeling very adventurous and may surprise you by taking a gamble near Mabon.

Time seems to move faster than ever during October. An exceptional number of cardinal sign planets create the need to juggle several projects at once. This trend peaks near the Full Moon on October 14. From All Hallows through November 16 Mars forms favorable aspects to several water and earth sign planets. You'll restore stability and feel more in control. There's time for a romantic encounter or a favorite leisure activity. At the end of November, Pluto enters Capricorn, joining Venus and Jupiter in your relationship sector. Partnerships enter a phase of intensity and transformation. You discover much about others and how they feel toward you. Keep an open mind and seek the truth, then all will be well. Attend to legal matters promptly.

December accents health and fitness. Prepare a healing ritual at the Full Moon on December 12 and another during the winter solstice. The quiet and cool evening hours will have a rejuvenating power. A health challenge can be overcome. During January, Mars and other Capricorn transits, including the Sun, are in opposition aspect to you. Adopt a live-and-let-live attitude toward others. Make few demands, and seek no favors. A strong sense of competition is present. Negotiate to avoid conflict. The Full Moon on January 10 falls in Cancer. It brings new insights about yourself. Meditate on self-love and acceptance by moonlight.

From Candlemas through Valentine's Day Mercury is in direct motion in your relationship sector. Get partners talking, and be a good listener. Someone close to you is making important decisions about the future. Jupiter, Mars, and Neptune cluster in your 8th house during February. Your interest in reincarnation is sparked. A spirit guide can be introduced in a dream. At the same time Venus begins a long passage through your career sector. This lasts through winter's end. Friends are willing to give your career a boost. Exercising creativity and artistic skills can lead to great professional success. On March 9 Mercury dovetails into a benevolent trine to your Sun. Winter's waning days find Mars following suit. Successful travel plans can be finalized. Your health and vitality are improving. Much healing, on many levels, is in process.

HEALTH

From springtime until early January, Jupiter, which rules your health sector, is in opposition to your Sun. The Sun is the source of life and vitality. This means that care must be taken to avoid those who are ill or who constitute an energy drain. Be cautious about acting upon health-related advice. Check with your own intuition and seek a second opinion if you're uncertain. The late winter favors healing and brings the promise of renewed strength.

LOVE

Your entire concept of partnerships and commitments is beginning a cycle of transformation and growth. Mysterious, intense Pluto and generous Jupiter will move through your 7th house of relationships. The Full Moon in Capricorn on July 18 marks a turning point in matters of the heart. Past life situations can explain love connections which seem especially karmic.

SPIRITUALITY

Early spring begins and late winter ends with Mercury conjunct Uranus in your sector of spiritual awareness. This suggests a beginning and ending involving spiritual quests. You could leave a coven or tradition that you've outgrown and seek new truths. A well-traveled and well-read acquaintance can serve as your inspiration, your spiritual counselor, or guru.

FINANCE

All four eclipses this year affect your finances. They all fall in your 2nd and 8th houses. Eclipses bring surprises and change. An established source of income can be replaced by new opportunity. Investments, inheritances, or insurance settlements could affect your security. August, January, and February will bring the specifics to light.

LEO

The year ahead for those
born under the sign of the Lion
July 23–August 22

Vivacious, dramatic, and self-expressive, Leo is ruled by the Sun and represented by the Lion. Comfortable being the center of attention, you are a born entertainer and leader. Sundays are your most fortunate days. Try to make purchases and move forward with ventures on Sundays to assure luck and success.

Spring begins on a subtle note, for water sign transits are stirring your 12th and 8th houses. You are acting with uncharacteristic secrecy. A love situation is complex near All Fool's Day. The New Moon on April 5 in Aries, your sister fire sign, augurs a fresh start. Frustrations will melt away. The next day Venus changes signs and begins a favorable aspect to Pluto and to your Sun. By May Eve harmony is restored. On May 10 Mars enters Leo, where it will remain in conjunction with your Sun through the end of June. This is a cycle of higher energy leading to much accomplishment. Direct anger and impatience into constructive venues and the world will be at your feet.

At the summer solstice a Mars-Neptune opposition can bring an encounter with the fey ones. Call out. Don't be surprised when Puck and the fairies answer. On July 13 a wonderful Venus transit through Leo commences. In the weeks leading up to your birthday, love and opportunity surround you. The good times roll on through Lammastide when Venus hovers near the solar eclipse in your sign. Bless a personal good luck talisman. Your priorities and desires are in flux from August 1 until the next eclipse on August 16. It will be a wild but interesting two weeks. Decide what it is that you really want and pursue it. There are endings and beginnings in process.

September begins with strong 3rd house sextile aspects involving Mars, Mercury, and Venus. You are open to learning. Welcome variety in daily routine. Juggle several projects at once. There's great versatility present. Read the newspaper and watch the news. Headlines are significant. After the autumnal equinox Mercury begins a retrograde cycle. It's important to remain well informed and to communicate with clarity through mid-October. Call ahead to avoid taking a wasted journey. Romantic prospects are wonderful near Samhain. Venus brightens your love and pleasure sector from October 19 – November 12. Plans for a handfasting could be discussed. Your gestures are welcomed and rewarded.

A favorable Mars influence is present from mid-November through Yuletide. Competitive activities are exhilarating. Your work load is lighter. The winter holidays offer extra time for recreation. As January begins, Jupiter makes a sign change and enters your sector of relationships. Talented and powerful people are drawing closer to you. The promise of partnerships which are sources of growth and opportunity is very real. The Aquarius eclipse of January 26 conjoins Jupiter. It can bring the specifics into focus. At Candlemas Venus moves into Aries, creating a benevolent aspect involving your 9th house. Spiritual and academic activities are enjoyable and carry the added boon of happy social connections throughout the rest of the winter.

February and March favor travel and serious writing. The Full Moon eclipse in Leo on February 9 is a time to be flexible and observant. Watch which way the wind blows before making a move. Honor the lunar eclipse by studying keepsake photographs and meditating on a happy childhood recollection. During March both Mars and Jupiter are in opposition aspect to you. Be aware of peer pressure and how the company you keep is affecting you. Associates may exhibit a zest for life. Enjoy the company of those who live on the edge, but don't allow your own balance to be upset. On March 14 Mars joins Uranus, Mercury, and the Sun in your 8th house. This favors research and truth seeking. As winter wanes, evidence of the afterlife can be present. Unspoken communication makes you aware that there is more going on than is first apparent.

HEALTH
Two of the eclipses are in Leo this year and highlight your 1st house. This means that your body and health conditions are in flux. Schedule regular dental and eye checkups. Network with new healthcare professionals. Health consultants you've seen previously might not be available. Weather and other environmental factors can affect your health. Focus on keeping your surroundings wholesome and being comfortable.

LOVE
A change of heart and loyalties may be brewing during August or January. Eclipses impact your 7th house of relationships at those times. Pluto impacts your 5th house from June 15 – November 26. You'll be aware of the transforming and healing power of love then. Soul mates are technically those whom we've encountered in previous incarnations. A transformative connection with a soul mate can occur during that period. The encounter will speak to your deepest heartfelt yearnings.

SPIRITUALITY
The planet Mars has a natural link with your 9th house of spirituality. This reveals that crusading for worthwhile causes and debating about spiritual topics make you receptive to deeper truths. The New Moon of April 5 is in your 9th house. This creates deep spiritual awareness. Explore the Native American, Vedic, and Celtic traditions during the four weeks following that lunation. Springtime brings you an awakening of higher consciousness.

FINANCE
Sober Saturn sits in your 2nd house of finances throughout the year. Time and patience are essential. Diligence on your part, rather than seeking a quick windfall, will pave the route to success. Appreciate all you have. Live within your means and don't overextend or make a risky change in your source of income.

VIRGO

*The year ahead for those
born under the sign of the Virgin*
August 23 – September 22

Thoughtful, discriminating, and particular, Virgo often seems aloof and reserved. However, those born under this sign harbor a deep inner sensitivity. Your emblem is the Virgin, suggesting purity and humanity. Your planet is the cosmic communicator, Mercury. Wednesday is your luckiest day each week for making decisions and starting new ventures.

Spring's earliest days find Uranus, Mercury, and Venus in your 7th house of partnership. From the vernal equinox through the New Moon on April 5, allow others to express individuality while discussing plans. Remind yourself to be tolerant. You can learn a great deal by being a good listener. From All Fool's Day until May 9, Mars hovers in your 11th house, in aspect to your Sun. Friends suggest worthwhile plans and ideas. Become active in groups and community matters.

Mid-May finds Venus and the Sun in Taurus creating a wonderful pair of trine aspects. Your 9th house is highlighted. Travel would be enjoyable and rewarding. Intimate relationships have a philosophical bent, they uplift and inspire you. May ends with Mercury turning retrograde in Gemini. Career situations can be frustrating through the summer solstice, but don't change jobs. Double-check directions and be patient. The light of the Capricorn Full Moon on July 18 illuminates new prospects. A problem is resolved. Near Lammastide the stars favor retreat and contemplation. A grouping of Leo planets in your 12th house brings out the lone wolf side of your nature. A solitary walk in the wilderness or time spent in reverie with just a few companions helps you to heal and focus. August 6-29 finds Venus brightening your personal life as it moves rapidly through your sign. Your artistic talents are in top form. Practice playing an instrument or create a drawing. Your sense of style and people skills are also excellent. Network. Nurture a promising new relationship.

September begins with Mars in your money sector. You'll work hard for security. Thoughts mostly revolve around earning power. Shop for an item you've long coveted in the days before Mabon. The yearned-for treasure may soon be your own. On September 25 Mercury begins a retrograde cycle in your 2nd house of finances which lasts until mid-October. Study your habits regarding money. Keep receipts: a purchase might have to be exchanged. You could return to an old job or revive a skill that was lucrative in the past. As All Hallows nears, Venus joins Pluto in your home and family sector. Bonds with loved ones intensify. It's a wonderful time to repair or improve a dwelling. During the chill November evenings simmer a harvest vegetable stew to serve guests.

From November 16 – December 6 Venus joins Jupiter in your sector of romance and happiness. A very joyful cycle regarding your social life commences. If you've dreamed of pursuing a new avocation or hobby, now is the time to do so. You may meet with unexpected success. As Yuletide approaches first Mercury, then Mars will affect your 4th house. A residential move is possible. There can be some stress involving relatives. Mercury is favorably aspected as December ends. Differences are resolved through discussion or letters.

January begins with Jupiter moving into your house of health, where it remains for an entire year. Let your New Year's resolutions address health and fitness goals. Your health and strength are good during January, but be aware of how old habits come into play. Mercury is retrograde most of January, turning direct near Candlemas. February 2 – 14 favors vacation travel. Communication with the very young or the elderly is excellent. During the remainder of February several Aquarius transits, including Neptune, Jupiter, Mars, and Mercury cluster in your 6th house. A special animal companion provides comfort and company. Your daily work is rewarding and interesting. The Full Moon on March 10 falls in your sign and is tinged by Saturn. You'll be thinking of how best to manage your time and resources. Needed materials and supplies can become available. Winter's final days find Mars joining the Sun and Uranus in your sector of relationships. A competitive note is present. Dynamic and original individuals impress you.

HEALTH
Eclipses on August 16 and January 26 activate your health sector. Be aware of changes in your health care needs. Investigate new health care options. Innovative techniques can be helpful, but be well informed. Saturn is in your sign all year. Be patient regarding health-related goals. You might need extra rest. Your family health history can be a significant factor impacting your health.

LOVE
Pluto flirts with the cusp of your 5th house of love all year. Review the myth of Demeter, Pluto, and Persephone, for it is rich in truths related to your own current love situation. Matters of the heart are most promising during May and August, when Venus aspects are excellent.

SPIRITUALITY
The eclipses of August 1 and February 9 are buried deep in your 12th house of solitude and the subconscious. Quiet meditation sessions and dream analysis can provide spiritual awakening. Acquire enhanced spiritual insights by visiting an area where you sense a past life was lived.

FINANCE
Jupiter, the celestial bringer of riches, favorably aspects your Sun from Ostara until early January. Earth signs are involved. Opportunities to add to your security are promising. Since the 5th house is involved an element of good luck prevails regarding finance. From November 14 – 25 Jupiter will trine Saturn which is conjunct your Sun. This has been called "the millionaire's aspect." Be alert. Fortune smiles especially at that time.

LIBRA

The year ahead for those
born under the sign of the Scales
September 23 – October 23

Symbolized by the Scale and ruled by Venus, Libras respect justice and always seek balance. Romantic, peaceful, and focused on sharing as well as partnership, your lucky day each week is Friday. Overcome your natural tendency to vacillate. Make your decisions and start projects on Fridays whenever possible to assure success.

Spring's earliest days find both Mercury and Venus in your health sector. Select a program of exercise and health care to assure wellness all year. From April 6 – May 9 Mars is powerfully aspected by both Jupiter and the Sun in your fellow cardinal signs. Your 10th house of career is involved. Prepare for some heavy competition. Direct energy constructively and keep trying. Professional aspirations are very important. Pursue a goal which nurtures your creative and spiritual needs while weighing financial considerations. Just after Beltane, Mercury begins a long passage through Gemini which lasts until July 10. This positive influence highlights your 9th house and favors travel. It's a perfect time to plan a spiritual pilgrimage. Studies will progress well too. While Mercury is retrograde May 27 – June 20, return to old haunts or try past life regression. Midsummer's

Day is perfect for releasing old patterns and making plans to journey onward and upward on many levels.

During July, Mars joins Saturn in your 12th house, where it will remain until August 19. Although you usually dislike being alone, this trend finds you tending to withdraw for some solitary reflection. Avoid large crowds and groups near the solar eclipse at Lammastide. Honor the early harvest with a personal ritual. Ecological concerns can interest you, as earth signs are involved. August ends on a bright note, as Venus enters your sign and stays until September 23. This ushers in a cycle of great happiness. Reach out to those you care about, visit an art display, or complete creative projects. The New Moon in Libra on September 29 is applying toward conjunctions with both Mars and retrograde Mercury. Get all of the facts before acting. Patience is a must. Call ahead before embarking on a journey. After October 16 the confusion clears.

Through All Hallows you'll express ideas eloquently and have a special ability to solve problems by compromise. From November 5 – 23 your 2nd house of finance and earning power is emphasized by Scorpio transits which favorably aspect Uranus. Innovation and sudden opportunities add to your income. At Thanksgiving you will have much to be grateful for. As December begins, the cosmic benefics, Venus and Jupiter, bless your home and family life. Make decisions about your living arrangements and real estate investments. Entertain at home and decorate your dwelling lavishly for Yule.

January is all about your favorite subject, romance. A stellium of

Aquarius planets, including Mercury, Jupiter, and Neptune, gather in your 5th house of pleasure. Pursue a new hobby; focus on exploring what true love really means to you. The eclipse on January 26 brings turning points in matters of the heart. Candlemas finds Mercury and Mars joining Pluto to form a square aspect to your Sun. Seek inner harmony and release stress. A relative might need assistance; a building can require maintenance. Take sensible safety precautions and all will be well. February finds Venus beginning a long passage through your 7th house, a trend which lasts through winter's end. Partnership, promises, and propriety are a focus. You might be drawn to study law and ethics on some level. From Valentine's Day through early March, Mercury joins other favorable Aquarius transits including Neptune. This cycle favors creative work, time spent with children, and declaring your love. On March 7 Venus, your ruler, begins a rare retrograde pattern. Be tolerant of others' idiosyncrasies as winter wanes. Reconsider business decisions. Treasure the bird in hand over the one in the bush.

HEALTH

The health of others can affect your own well-being this year. Saturn in Virgo will oppose Uranus in your 6th house. Avoid those whom you can't help but who consistently make demands, and those who are obviously showing cold and flu symptoms. Your health is subject to rapid changes now. Rest and recoup if you feel under the weather. You'll soon be up and well again.

LOVE

The August 16 and January 26 eclipses bring surprises involving your 5th house of love. You can discover new qualities within a present relationship or experience a new attraction to an exciting acquaintance. Neptune is involved, so love's magic has a mystical quality. Don't change your commitment status after March 7 when Venus goes retrograde.

SPIRITUALITY

The total eclipse at Lammastide affects your choice of spiritual traditions. You might want to explore the teachings of a new coven or meditation circle. Be open to new paths. They can reward you by opening new doorways to higher awareness. A friend suggests a rewarding path of spirituality near the time of the February 9 eclipse. Ignite a pale blue or ivory taper at Candlemas and request that the Lord and Lady illuminate your spiritual path.

FINANCE

Pluto, ruler of your 2nd house of cash flow, enters Capricorn this year. You are beginning a long-term phase when home and family related expenses will have to be considered. Don't overextend regarding hefty real estate investments. Money matters will improve dramatically when Jupiter enters Aquarius in early January. When Venus, ruler of your 8th house, goes retrograde in March be careful of business partnerships and financial schemes suggested by others. Your own business judgment is better than the advice offered by others during late winter.

SCORPIO

The year ahead for those
born under the sign of the Scorpion
October 24–November 21

Intense and determined, you will always emphasize that which is truly meaningful. The Scorpion scorns shallowness in any form. Co-ruled by Mars and Pluto, your lucky day each week is Tuesday. Secrets (a favorite subject of yours) are revealed and favorable opportunities arise when you make decisions on Tuesdays.

Springtime begins with happy chatter. Mercury conjoins Venus and Uranus in your sector of love and pleasure. A sense of discovery and novelty is pervasive throughout early April. The New Moon on April 5 accents health and fitness. Plan a blessing for good health on May Eve. Through May 9 energetic Mars makes a favorable trine aspect to your Sun, promising tremendous strength and vitality. Since your 9th house is involved, your sense of adventure deepens. You'll yearn to wander and explore. On May 19 the Full Moon in Scorpio is tinged by a Neptune square. Mercury is about to turn retrograde while making a quincunx aspect. Dreams and visions must not be taken literally. Direct your heightened imagination and creativity into constructive pursuits through the month's end.

During the weeks preceding Midsummer's Day, Gemini transits, including the Sun, Venus, and retrograde Mercury, highlight your 8th house of mysteries and the afterlife. A past life memory can come to light; spirits from other dimensions communicate. Fate intervenes in plans, so be flexible and observant. In July, Mars enters your 11th house where it conjoins Saturn in Virgo. Group activities provide challenges all month. Use caution in committing to plans. The eclipse on Lammas dramatically affects your 10th house of career and recognition. Your field of expertise is changing. You might abandon one career in favor of something new. The lunar eclipse on the 16th impacts home and family life. A residential move can be considered, and family dynamics are shifting.

September is a time for rest and reverie, with a stellium of Libra planets in your sector of solitude and subconscious yearnings. Take note of dreams near the autumnal equinox. Answers come from within. Allow nature and wildlife to draw nigh. The natural world offers peace and comfort. October finds Venus and Mars in your sign. Social prospects are especially bright as Samhain nears. Adorn yourself. Assemble an especially wonderful costume for Halloween parties and rituals. Initiative is strong. Much can be accomplished near your birthday. The New Moon on October 28 brings a deeper understanding of your own psyche. Mercury moves rapidly through Scorpio from November 5 – 23. This is wonderful for travel, study, and analysis of all kinds.

November finds Pluto, your ruler, completing a sign change as it moves into Capricorn, where it will remain for many years. This affects your 3rd house.

A sibling or neighbor is changing. Don't be in denial when obvious signs are being sent. Transportation needs are being considered and information exchange is very important. Be alert and stay well informed and all will be well. Pluto's influence promises to be a positive one, for it is well aspected.

Venus begins a passage through your home and family sector on December 8, where it will remain through New Year's Day. Entertain at home, and honor the traditions of the season. Art, music, good company, and revelry rule. January finds Mars making several important aspects in your 3rd house, including a Saturn opposition. Be diplomatic when discussing controversial issues. Call ahead and confirm plans. Just after Candlemas, Mercury turns direct and any confusion will clear. Bless a crystal of citrine or aquamarine at the sabbat to carry as a charm to protect communication and transportation through the winter's end. On February 3 Venus enters your 6th house where it remains through March. Developing more rapport with either a domestic or wild creature can heal you. On March 15 Mars creates a positive influence for both love and creativity. Your vitality and motivation will be especially high during the last days of winter.

HEALTH

Fiery Mars and Aries rule your health sector. Healing rituals using candles dedicated to well-being can always be helpful. The combination of color, light, and heat can stimulate your recovery. You have scant patience with illness. Remember to allow enough time to heal when you are under the weather.

April 2008 and February-March 2009 find Venus in your health sector. Your health improves during those times.

LOVE

Unpredictable Uranus has been in your love sector for several years. Relationships have been subject to sudden change. Balancing love and intimacy with freedom and independence has been a focus. Dedicate the Mabon sabbat to a love rite, for Venus enters your sign in late September. Brew a true love herbal tea using rose petals, mint, and lemon verbena. Sip it during the weeks just before your birthday. The stars promise happiness in matters of the heart as Halloween approaches.

SPIRITUALITY

The Moon has a powerful impact on your spiritual awakening, because Moon-ruled Cancer oversees your 9th house. Learn more about lunar deities. Try forming a meditation circle to meet at New and Full Moons each month. Practice drawing down the Moon. The New Moon on July 2 and the Full Moon on January 10 mark times when Luna's lyrics will sing most sweetly to your spirit.

FINANCE

During recent years economic conditions which seemed beyond your control have affected your finances. Pluto is moving away from your financial sector, promising a time of more peace and security. Moneymaking ideas as well as studies can enhance your earning power most of the year. Generous Jupiter makes a benevolent sextile to your Sun from springtime through early January.

SAGITTARIUS

The year ahead for those
born under the sign of the Archer
November 22 – December 21

Friendly and idealistic, you cherish independence. A child of expansive Jupiter, you are a wanderer and adventurer. Thursday is your lucky day each week for finalizing plans and making choices.

Spring finds your career aspirations at a turning point. Retrograde Saturn is perched at your midheaven. Questions of competence and credibility arise near All Fool' s Day. At the same time, Venus brightens your 4th house. Your home becomes a peaceful haven for problem solving. From April 7 – May Eve your 5th house of pleasure and romance is highlighted by several Aries transits. The Maypole dance connects you with a charming admirer.

On May 9 Mars enters Leo where it aspects your 9th house favorably through July 1, underscoring a genuine zest for life. You'll be ready for journeys and adventures of all kinds, with the added blessing of great physical vitality. Enter contests and competitions near June 18 when the Full Moon shines in your sign. From mid-July through Lammastide, Venus trines your Sun. Creativity and charm abound. Travel would be enriching and rewarding during late July, especially if you're able to travel abroad.

Five different planetary transits impact your career sector at various times in August. The entire month is all about professional aspirations and your ambitions. You'll attract attention. Pursue opportunities which showcase your capabilities. During September, Jupiter completes its retrograde in your 2nd house. Old financial obligations or debts are becoming more manageable. You're entering a more promising security cycle. A pay raise is possible. After Mabon a retrograde Mercury in Libra transit affects your 11th house. The trend lasts through October 16. A reunion with a longtime friend is likely. Enjoy chance meetings with those from your past. You may reconsider the pursuit of a dream once abandoned. The days before Halloween are a time for rest and reflection. Scorpio transits in your 12th house encourage you to withdraw. Get in touch with your inner voice for direction.

The Samhain sabbat finds Venus conjunct your Sun. This is a happy pattern which lasts through November 12. Circulate and socialize; purchase new fashions. Revel in the goodness you're attracting. A positive and nurturing relationship bonds. Commitment grows. From late November through December 27 Mars races through your sign, adding fire and excitement. Curb anger, though. Patiently direct valuable energy into constructive ends. Much can be accomplished near your birthday. At Yuletide the Sun joins Mercury and Pluto in your 2nd house of finances. Prepare a sachet of prosperity herbs, including bayberry leaves, basil, and cinnamon, to bless your workplace. Address financial desires in making spiritual petitions.

On January 4 Venus joins Uranus in your home and family sector, a trend which lasts through Candlemas. It's a wonderful time to redecorate, plan home improvements, and to foster a deeper sense of unity with both relatives and members of your extended family. Genealogical study could uncover interesting surprises. From January 28 – February 14 Mercury dips into your 2nd house. Learn more about financial management. Don't repeat financial patterns and habits which led to previous disappointments. Conversations about monetary matters are enlightening.

Late February finds Aquarius transits including Neptune, Jupiter, and Mars clustered in sextile aspect to your Sun. Don't neglect correspondence. Return all calls and answer letters promptly. Get organized. Commuter travel and multitasking might be necessary. Yes, you can get everything done. Time passes more quickly than usual. During March, Venus turns retrograde in your 5th house of romantic love. Don't change your commitment status at present. Be friendly and tolerant of the foibles of a loved one. A change of heart may be followed by regrets. Don't be impulsive in love as winter wanes. Smile and be tolerant if someone displays eclectic preferences in art and music which you can't appreciate.

HEALTH
Sensual (and stubborn) Taurus rules your 6th house of health. Always maintain good health habits. Splurge only occasionally on sweets and other forbidden goodies. The healing companionship offered by a beloved pet or time spent in serene outdoor settings can be especially helpful to you. Avoid noise pollution. Harsh voices and loud music or industrial racket can make you feel unwell.

LOVE
The Full Moon on October 14 ushers in a four-week cycle of wisdom and illumination regarding love. The element fire rules your 5th house of love. You often begin and end a romance suddenly. Candle-burning rituals can draw happiness in matters of the heart. Always burn two tapers or votives, one colored red and the other pink or coral. This represents you and your intended. Position the lit flames side by side. Address a request to Venus for true love to be rewarded.

SPIRITUALITY
The Sun has a special link with your 9th house. Explore the traditions behind the great solar festivals of earlier times. Then incorporate the ancient ways into your personal rituals at Ostara, Litha, Mabon, and Yule. Add a Sun picture or plaque with a wise and benevolent face at its center to your sacred space.

FINANCE
This year Pluto, which has been flirting with the cusp of your 2nd house of finances for some time, makes the leap for the long haul. Pluto changes signs only once in a generation or so. This takes place at the end of November. Your values and financial priorities are in a state of transformation. Seek ways to turn antiques, investments, a hobby, or a natural aptitude into a source of ready cash. Generous Jupiter remains in your financial sector from spring until early January. Overall, this bodes well for your money matters.

CAPRICORN
The year ahead for those
born under the sign of the Goat
December 22 – January 19

Capricorn, the zodiac's responsible achiever, is symbolized by the steady and sure-footed Goat. You are persistent yet cautious, and possess a subtle and wry sense of humor. Sober Saturn is your ruler and Saturday is your lucky day each week. Make both business and personal decisions on Saturdays to assure optimum success.

Spring begins with dynamic Mars opposing your birth sign. Exciting individuals make plans for you. Cooperate. Make no demands. A legal matter might need attention. Prepare rituals for peace and harmony at the vernal equinox. On May 9 expect a major shift in the cosmic energies. Mars changes signs and Jupiter is turning retrograde. It's a time of revision and second chances. Reflect upon what has been traditional. Old patterns reveal future truths. A hobby or sport brings pleasure and happiness while the springtime warms and brightens.

June finds planets in Gemini and Leo making a double quincunx aspect to your Sun. This creates a rare Yod or "Eye of God" pattern impacting you through the summer solstice. Fate is at work in your life. Some things just are or are not meant to be. Appreciate synchronicities and you'll be guided to manifest what's best. Go with the flow. Heed omens from animal guides. On July 2 Mars joins Saturn in Virgo. Both planets favorably aspect your Sun through mid-August. Your energy level is especially high. It's a wonderful influence for taking on a challenge. Consider long distance travel or programs of higher education. The Capricorn Full Moon of July 18 puts you in tune with your own potentials. Honor the lunation by preparing a talisman to enhance personal charisma and confidence. From August 6 – 30 a Venus aspect promises heightened creativity. Romantic feelings develop toward those who stimulate your intellect and curiosity.

September brings you greater visibility at work. A stellium of planets group in your 10th house of fame and fortune during the three weeks before the autumnal equinox. Communication skills are an asset to your professional situation because Mercury is prominent. You might travel or multitask in connection with your work through October. As Samhain nears, Venus joins Pluto in your 12th house. Involvement in charities and volunteer work would bring you deep personal satisfaction. From November 5-21 Mercury transits your 11th house. Friends offer valuable new ideas during the course of casual conversations. Consider becoming more active within groups. In mid-November, Venus enters your sign, where it moves into conjunction with Jupiter. Thanksgiving season brings a cycle of growth and opportunity. Accept and issue invitations. November ends with deep and mysterious Pluto entering your sign where it will remain for many years. You'll discover new aptitudes and personal potentials. Past life memories arise from dream analysis and meditation.

Mercury enters your sign on December 12. Opportunities for travel come through New Year's Eve. The right decisions are made and puzzles are solved. Your mind is bright, and insight is in peak form. The Capricorn New Moon on December 27 favors a fresh start. Sow and nurture all that you wish to grow during the year ahead. Enthusiasm and a competitive mood prevail during January. Dynamic Mars races through your sign all month. Carry a lodestone or tiger's eye agate to help channel impatience and anger into constructive avenues. Since Mars makes powerful aspects to both Saturn and the Sun, you will grow a great deal. Use your time and resources efficiently. By Candlemas a favor is returned, for Mercury completes a retrograde in your sign. The first half of February brings interesting messages. You may be packing for a journey by the time of the eclipse on February 9. In late February planets in Aquarius impact your 2nd house of finances. Imaginative plans increase your earnings. A hunch as well as new developments in your field lead to worthwhile new opportunities. On March 7 Venus turns retrograde in your home and family sector. Be careful not to discard memorabilia and keepsakes impulsively. During March tense family situations from the past are resolved.

HEALTH
Saturn, your ruler, will be in health-conscious Virgo all year where it favorably aspects your Sun. This is a very positive influence for developing good health habits and for recovering from any ongoing health challenges.

LOVE
Prepare a wildflower bouquet on May Day. Offer it to the one whom you would woo. Venus smiles on your love sector during May. Saturn and Jupiter offer support with a benevolent grand trine pattern. Friday, November 13, brings a Full Moon in your 5th house of romance. Love prospects should improve by Thanksgiving.

SPIRITUALITY
Saturn hovers in Virgo, your 9th house of spirituality, all year. This favors drawing upon the most ancient Earth deities. The Full Moon on March 10 marks a time of significant spiritual focus. Journey to a sacred mountain or study films and photos of sacred peaks. Armchair travel can be equally effective if an actual trek isn't feasible. Collect powerful stones to surround a home altar or fire circle. Garnet, hematite, obsidian, jet, and apache tear would be good choices.

FINANCE
All four of the eclipses this year fall in your 2nd and 8th houses. This relates directly to finances. Prepare for surprises. A different source of income and new financial plans are emerging. August as well as late January through mid-February will bring the specifics into focus. Since lucky Jupiter brightens your sign from Ostara throughout Yuletide, there should be ample opportunities to add to your income. A desirable standard of living, with plenty of creature comforts, is assured.

AQUARIUS

The year ahead for those
born under the sign of the Water Bearer
January 20–February 18

Unpredictable and detached, you forever astound and intrigue others. Uranus, the planet of innovation and freedom, is your ruler. Saturdays are your luckiest day each week. Make purchases and begin journeys or projects then.

At the vernal equinox Venus and Mercury cluster with Uranus in your sector of finances. Conversation will be focused on generating income. Promising opportunities for rewarding employment arise near All Fool's Day. Through the first week of May, Mars impacts your 6th house. Release stress and anger; it can impact your health. Animal companions are a source of both love and concern. Bless a favorite treat at the Beltane sabbat and offer it to the animals who brighten your life. A tiny crystal can be consecrated and added to the collar or cage of an animal friend to strengthen the bond between you.

During June, Mercury, ruler of your 5th house of romance, is retrograde in Gemini. This promises reunions with lost loves. Loyalties and attachments are in flux. Be sensitive to repeating patterns involving heart connections. At Midsummer's Eve the tide turns. From June 20 – July 10 decisions and love commitments are favored. Communication with those near and dear

is excellent. From the last half of July through mid-August, Leo transits affect your 7th house. Companions offer suggestions. Revel in the attraction of opposites. The solar eclipse of August 1 reveals much about a close partner. Prepare a talisman to assure justice and maintain balance at Lammas. The lunar eclipse on August 16 in your sign conjoins fanciful, imaginative Neptune. Reality is clouded. If in doubt, wait for the facts to be revealed before making choices. A sense of the miraculous prevails through month's end.

Venus, Mercury, and Mars aspect your 9th house favorably as September begins. Air travel is favored, as are journeys of the mind and spirit. There is much to learn. If you've always yearned to write, now is the time to jot down those jokes, stories, and poems. From the autumnal equinox through October 3, Mars sextiles Pluto and simultaneously trines your Sun. Expect an increase in energy and motivation. Much can be accomplished. Take time to exercise. From October 19 – November 12 Venus joins Pluto in your sector or friendships and goals. Acquaintances inspire you. At All Hallows cast a ceremonial circle for friendship. Light individual votive candles from a single, central flame and then place them in a circle to represent a group bond that is eternal.

At the end of November, Uranus completes its retrograde. Old business is concluded. Prepare to move forward. All that is ultramodern impresses you as Yuletide approaches. On December 8 Venus enters your sign, ushering in a time of happiness and social activity which lasts through January 3. The holiday season is one of wish fulfillment. Early January begins a yearlong Jupiter transit in your sign. There's an increasing urge to grow on many levels as your birthday nears. Consider options with care and do research while Mercury retrogrades toward your 12th house from January 12 – February 2. Center Candlemas rites on healing of both the body and soul.

From February 5 – March 14 Mars enters Aquarius, where it conjoins Jupiter, Neptune, and Mercury. This planetary powerhouse ushers in an eventful time. You'll shatter old barriers and implement constructive changes. The February 9 eclipse accents partnerships. Don't resist inevitable change; people will enter and leave your life. Allow others to grow and explore through the month's end. March finds Venus retrograde in your 3rd house. Relationships with siblings and neighbors can be demanding. Be patient. Undercurrents and extenuating circumstances are afoot. As winter ends, facts come to light. You'll be glad that you were understanding and tolerant.

HEALTH
The eclipses on August 16 and January 26 conjoin your Sun, indicating changes in your vitality and health care needs. Experiment with alternative care programs. The Neptune influence which comes with the August 16 pattern can point to a misdiagnosis, allergies, and food sensitivities. Get a second opinion if there is uncertainty. The January solar eclipse conjoins Jupiter. This is spectacular for healing. Health goals, including the proper weight, can be attained.

LOVE
The August 1 and February 9 south node eclipses activate your 7th house of relationships. Closest ties will demand effort and energy. Offer those you care most about emotional support. Adjustments are needed concerning the status quo. It's a time of endings and beginnings. The Full Moon on December 12 highlights your sector of romance. On that day select a fragrant red apple and stud it with cloves to make a pomander. Concentrate on true love. Tie the pomander with golden ribbons and a sprig of mistletoe. Suspend it in your favorite place. Love will soon draw nigh.

SPIRITUALITY
From August 20 – October 3 Mars sweeps through your 9th house of spirituality. Various other planets, including Mercury, join the parade during late summer and early autumn. This favors sacred travel and spiritual studies. It's a perfect time to seek teaching from a guru, high priestess, or shaman. Your personal motivation and enthusiasm contribute to the success of your spiritual quest.

FINANCE
From the vernal equinox through April 6 and again January 4 – February 2, Venus conjoins Uranus in your financial sector. Sudden profits, windfalls, and opportunities are possible. For many years Uranus has created unrest and uncertainty regarding finances. You might have literally gone from rags to riches and back again more than once. In January, when generous Jupiter enters your sign, a rewarding year of greater overall prosperity commences. Smile.

PISCES

The year ahead for those
born under the sign of the Fish
February 19 – March 20

The nature of Pisces is compassionate and visionary. Dreamy, impressionable Neptune is your ruling planet, revealing a link with the glamorous Lord of the Seas. Thursday is your lucky day each week for finalizing all business and personal decisions.

Springtime emphasizes journeys. Mercury races through your sign tagging Venus and Uranus until April 2. Expect some interesting conversations. New ideas are suggested and business combines gracefully with pleasure. Mars swims through Cancer, your sister water sign until May 9, enhancing your energy level. Romantic urges are pronounced, and you'll express your love. At Beltane plan a romantic stroll along the waterfront with one whom you find attractive. May Day's natural magic will work quickly to intensify the relationship.

From mid-May through June 18 your 4th house of residence and family life is highlighted. Home improvements and real estate transactions can be a focus. The New Moon on June 3 brings the specifics into focus. This is a wonderful time to facilitate better communication between both relatives and extended family members. At the summer solstice Venus enters your 5th house of love and pleasure, where it happily nurtures love connections through July 12.

Throughout July until August 18 Mars joins Saturn in your 7th house. A partner has expectations. A competitive mood prevails. Adapt and keep the peace. Follow directions; keep records and receipts. Questions of fairness and legality might have to be addressed. The eclipses of August highlight your 12th and 6th houses. Resist the temptation to be critical of coworkers. It's not the time to be a perfectionist. A new animal companion may enter your life. A deep appreciation for wild creatures and nature prevails. Late August and early September highlight your 8th house, the gateway to the afterlife. A mystery is solved; messages from beyond the veil offer closure.

The Full Moon of September 15 conjoins Uranus in your sign. A four-week time of self discovery commences. There is an urge to explore and to reclaim freedom. New technologies offer efficient help with projects. As October begins, Mars and Venus in Scorpio create a wholesome water sign aspect pattern. Your emotional balance is healthy. Affection and appreciation for grandparent/grandchild connections prevail. You will enjoy the cultural traditions of faraway lands. At Samhain place a world globe upon the altar. Ask the Lord and Lady for the blessing of world peace.

November accents career goals. Sagittarius transits move through your 10th house of fame and fortune. Early in the month a friend provides valuable career tips. After the 17th, planets in mutable signs will square Mars. You may seek a position of greater leadership. As the month ends Pluto enters your 11th house promising a revamping of goals and desires. Community life and politics interest you. December 8 finds Venus entering your 12th house where it aspects Neptune. Charity work brings deep happiness during the days before the winter solstice. Share your time and resources with those in need. You can make a real difference. On New Year's Eve, Saturn turns retrograde in your 7th house. The backward spin continues throughout the winter. A close companion repeats old patterns. Detach if you feel a relationship is draining you. Reclaiming your independence means salvation. Others are involved in their own needs for the time being. Quell demands and expectations.

On January 4 Venus enters Pisces and remains through Candlemas. Your artistic talents are blossoming. Dance, photography, and other forms of creative expression allow you to create beauty within and around you. Romantic prospects appear; you are at your most charming and charismatic. During February several planets, including Jupiter and Mars, gather in your 12th house. You will revel in peace and solitude. Dreams are meaningful. A past life recollection comes through meditation or dream analysis. On February 24 the New Moon in your sign brings a shift in your focus. Winter's final weeks find you more expressive and involved. On March 9 Mercury enters Pisces. This is intellectually stimulating. Conversations, travel, and plans for the future are in your thoughts.

HEALTH
Water revitalizes you. Try various types of immersion baths and saunas to see which are most helpful. Your lower extremities are always vulnerable. Treat your feet regularly to a warm, sudsy foot bath.

LOVE
The sentimental, sensitive influence of the Moon rules your love sector. Exchange scrapbook and photo albums which bring childhood memories to life in order to forge a deeper bond with a love interest. Prepare a family tree with anecdotes about keepsake heirlooms and favorite recipes attached. Share it with the one you care for. The Full Moon on January 10 is favorably aspected in your 5th house of romance. Reach out to strengthen a desired liaison at that time.

SPIRITUALITY
The August 16 north node eclipse conjoins Neptune, in your 12th house of the subconscious. Your natural intuition will be heightened during the twelve months following that eclipse. Your sixth sense is developing. Observe how you feel when a hunch turns out to be correct. That special feeling is called confirmation by psychics. Make notes of vivid dreams and impressions you receive. This will help you to use your valuable spiritual potentials effectively.

FINANCE
Hard angle aspects involving Uranus, Pluto, and Saturn in mutable signs have stressed your resources recently. Don't lend or give more to others than you can afford to spare. Those who seek your financial assistance can be offered help and encouragement in other ways. At the end of November, Pluto's sign change ushers in a more promising pattern for saving and acquiring future security.

Lincoln's Doppelganger

A QUEER DREAM or illusion had haunted Lincoln at times through the winter. On the evening of his election he had thrown himself on one of the haircloth sofas at home, just after the first telegrams of November 6 had told him he was elected President, and looking into a bureau mirror across the room he saw himself full length, but with two faces.

It bothered him; he got up; the illusion vanished; but when he lay down again there in the glass again were two faces, one paler than the other. He got up again, mixed in the election excitement, forgot about it; but it came back, and haunted him. He told his wife about it; she worried too.

A few days later he tried it once more and the illusion of the two faces again registered to his eyes. But that was the last; the ghost since then wouldn't come back, he told his wife, who said it was a sign he would be elected to a second term, and the death pallor of one face meant he wouldn't live through his second term.

– CARL SANDBURG, *Abraham Lincoln: The War Years*

Naming the Moons

Poetic readings by Pagans and Native Americans

LONG BEFORE SUN deities were worshipped, the Moon in all of her forms and phases was deified. The Full Moon each month marks the culmination of an energy cycle. Human emotions, plant and animal life, weather and tides are directly affected by lunar rhythms. Old World Pagans and Early Native Americans gave each Full Moon a name. In both cultures art, legends and poetry identified important events in each passing cycle. The Full Moon always takes place in the sign opposite the Sun's sign, symbolizing polarity and balance. During the course of the common calendar year thirteen Full Moons arise. The mystique surrounding the number thirteen further hints at the special magic of Moon lore.

We suggest that you meditate on these seasonal messages as you contemplate the beauty and wonder of the Full Moon throughout the year:

The Full Moon with Sun in Aries and Moon in Libra occurs between March 20 and April 19.

Pagan Seed Moon – This is a time to plant for growth within your own psyche as well as in the garden.

Native American Moon of the Budding Trees – Adventure and new growth are promised, but avoid rashness. The tree that buds too soon will be frozen.

Luna

*The Moon Woman of the
Haida Indians in British Columbia*

The Full Moon with Sun in Taurus and Moon in Scorpio occurs between April 20 and May 20.

Pagan Hare Moon – Images of the Easter Bunny represent vitality, creativity and reproduction.

Native American Moon of the Frog Birth – The abundance of tadpoles symbolizes the creation of new life. A time of love, passion and sensuality.

The Full Moon with Sun in Gemini and Moon in Sagittarius occurs between May 21 and June 21.

Pagan Dyad Moon – There are at least two sides to every story. Be fair and balanced. Consider the whole situation before choosing.

Native American Moon of the Corn – Cornfields were the heart of early villages, and with cultivation tribal culture took a leap forward. Corn, long cherished for its taste and versatility, is considered a symbol of intelligence. Dried kernels are used in blessing rituals.

The Full Moon with Sun in Cancer and Moon in Capricorn occurs between June 21 and July 22.

Pagan Mead Moon – A cycle of important work. Brewing for winter mead and ale begins and hay is mown. The phrase "make hay while the sun shines" was originally coined to describe this cycle.

Native American Strong Sun Moon – The life-giving Sun mingles with Moon's sensitive nurture to bring strength and growth.

The Full Moon with Sun in Leo and Moon in Aquarius occurs between July 23 and August 22.

Pagan Wort Moon – Various worts (an Old English term for plants) are gathered and preserved. A time of richness and early harvest.

Native American Moon of the Ripening Berries – Vibrant health and enhanced well-being are suggested. Rich in vitamin C, berries are prevalent in healing. Artistic endeavors are indicated; berries are used to create paints and dyes for textiles and pottery.

The Full Moon with Sun in Virgo and Moon in Pisces occurs between August 23 and September 22.

Pagan Barley Moon – Persephone carrying a sheaf of grain is the zodiacal depiction of Virgo. Pure harvest fruits carry the seeds of rebirth.

Native American Harvest Moon – Resources are drawn in and consolidated. It's time for cookery, neatness and craftsmanship.

The Full Moon with Sun in Libra and Moon in Aries occurs between September 23 and October 23.

Pagan Wine Blood Moon – Grapes are crushed and fermented. Animals were traditionally bled and sacrificed to provide food and clothing for the oncoming of winter.

Native American Moon of the Flying Ducks – Migration. The flocks set forth, seeking a better tomorrow in another place.

The Full Moon with Sun in Scorpio and Moon in Taurus occurs between October 24 and November 21.

Pagan Snow Moon – Early snow-flakes blow, heralding the cold and darkness. Life crystallizes, so warmth must be preserved.

Native American Moon of the First Freeze – Tales of valor and glory are exchanged around the evening fire to stave off concerns about the coming winter. Survival and heroism are encouraged.

The Full Moon with Sun in Sagittarius and Moon in Gemini occurs between November 22 and December 21.

Pagan Oak Moon – Amidst holiday revelry a Yule log is set aflame to celebrate warmth and light. Oak is preferred because it burns long and was originally sacred to Jove. The oak is also honored for its noble form and endurance in the face of icy blasts.

Native American Moon of the Blizzards – Good judgment, discretion, knowledge of one's self and circumstances are especially important. It's a competitive time with survival as the goal.

The Full Moon with Sun in Capricorn and Moon in Cancer occurs between December 22 and January 19

Pagan Wolf Moon – The fierce, hungrywolf wanders and forages now. The hunt goes on during the bleakest nights.

Native American Moon of Cleansing Renewal – Nature rests, guarding what has been gained. During winter's sleep, vital energy is replenished and cherished.

The Full Moon with Sun in Aquarius and Moon in Leo occurs between January 20 and February 18.

Pagan Storm Moon – A time to recognize how destructive anger can be. The quality of storms, in nature or in individuals, foretells the pattern of the coming year.

Native American Moon of Rest and Purification – Detoxify both body and mind. It's time to release worn-out possessions and dead-end relationships. Elimination and enough sleep promote good health.

The Full Moon with Sun in Pisces and Moon in Virgo occurs between February 19 and March 20.

Pagan Chastity Moon – Focus on spiritual cleansing in preparation for spring, including Lent. The stale cob-webs of winter are chased away with the traditions of spring cleaning.

Native American Big Wind Moon – The stress of winter is lifted. Change is coming. It's time to be receptive to new ideas and opportunities. Check the direction of the wind. Which way does it blow?

– ELAINE NEUMEIER

The Moon Rabbit of the Aztecs

The Book of Enoch

THE BOOK OF ENOCH is an ancient Jewish writing, regarded by some as a part of the Bible. Small fragments of it were found among the Dead Sea Scrolls in the caves at Qumran. It was written in Aramaic, but very early in the Christian era it was translated into Greek, and then into Latin. These translations are now lost. We know them only from a few quotations made by early Christian writers, including the author of one of the shorter books of the New Testament (Jude). A few centuries later the Book of Enoch was also translated into Ethiopic, for use of the Church of Ethiopia. That church – alone among all the ancient churches of Christendom! – has always considered it to be part of the Old Testament. This is why there are many manuscripts of the Book of Enoch in Ethiopic.

The Book of Enoch is not found in Western Bibles, whether Catholic or Protestant. In these Bibles Enoch himself is hardly mentioned. In Genesis (chapter 5) he figures as one of the ten patriarchs from Adam to Noah. Except for Enoch, these patriarchs all are said to have died only after lives of enormous length, from Methuselah's 969 years down to Lamech's 777 years. Only Enoch breaks the pattern. He is said to have lived on earth for just 365 years, and there is no mention of his death at all. Rather, we are told that "Enoch walked with God: and he was not; for God took him" (Genesis 5:24). These cryptic words are made clearer elsewhere in the Bible, where it is openly said that Enoch did not die, but was "translated," that is, he was taken up alive from the earth into the heavens (Hebrews 11:5; in Catholic Bibles also Ecclesiasticus 44:16, 49:14).

Descent of the Watchers

Behind these few words lies a whole back-story, which can be read in the Book of Enoch and in a few other ancient works such as the Book of Jubilees, the Book of the Secrets of Enoch, and the Hebrew Apocalypse of Enoch. In short, after Adam and Eve were expelled from the Garden of Eden, they and their descendants fell into impurity and corruption. In the days of Adam's great-great-great-grandson Jared, this corruption spread even to some of the angels who had been assigned to watch silently over mankind. In the year 1000 after the creation, being enticed by the beauty of mortal women, two hundred of these angelic Watchers came down from the heavens. This was the Descent of the Watchers, and it is mentioned even in our Western Bibles: "And it came to pass, when men began to multiply on the face of the earth, and daughters were born to them, that the sons of God saw the daughters of men that they were fair; and they took them wives of all which they chose" (Genesis 6:1-2).

To win human wives for themselves, as the Book of Enoch tells us, these Watchers taught women the arts of magic and the use of herbs and other plants. They also taught men the arts of smithcraft, how to make weapons and jewelry, as well as mineral dyes and cosmetics for women to use. They also taught people how to read the signs of the times in the heavens. Armed with all the fruits of this forbidden knowledge, mankind turned more and more toward violence and lust, bloodshed and impurity. As if that were not misery enough, from the union of women with these fallen Watchers there was born a race of mighty giants, towering lawless creatures whose hungers were insatiable, who finally began to devour even men and women. To remedy this, God sent four archangels to bind the fallen Watchers and to slay their offspring.

Only one man remained free from this corruption, pleasing God. He was Enoch, Jared's eldest son. (The name Jared is said by Hebrew scholars to mean "descent" in that language, and Enoch to mean "an initiate.") Enoch alone was spared death. Instead, he was taken up alive from the earth into the heavens when he was only 365 years old. (It is significant that this is also the number of days in a common year.)

Transfiguration

There Enoch was shown all the mysteries of cosmic order and the true calendar, all the heavens and the serried ranks of angels that dwelt in them, the spirits of mortals and their fates, and finally the shape of the history of the world from its creation to its final days. Even secrets hidden from the angels were revealed to him. He was also told what sentence had been passed upon the two hundred fallen Watchers and the giants who were their children.

Afterwards Enoch was sent back to earth for just a few weeks to tell his descendants what he had learned in the heavens, and to write books that would preserve these secrets for the sake of generations to come. Then he was taken back up into the heavens and was seen no more among men. There he remains, transfigured into the angel Metatron, the greatest of all the angels, who is next to God upon the heavenly throne.

Although the fallen Watchers had been imprisoned and the giants destroyed, men and women continued down the path of violence and lawlessness, making full use of all the forbidden arts and crafts, for several centuries longer. Only Enoch's descendants – his son Methuselah, his grandson Lamech, and his great-grandson Noah – cherished the lessons of Enoch and preserved his writings. Noah and his wife, with his three sons and their wives, survived the great flood, taking the writings of Enoch with them into the ark. In this way these books came safely through the flood. For this reason they were thought to be the oldest books in all the world.

– ROBERT MATHIESEN

109

The Moonstruck Ladle

ONCE UPON A TIME there lived a sly old woman adept at preying on others. She delighted in tricky schemes to separate her family and neighbors from their money. When her nephew married a simple country lass, Granny Greedle viewed the bride as a new pigeon. During her first visit, the old woman asked red-cheeked Letty if she was disturbed by the scratching in the walls. "What scratching?" the young woman asked. "I don't hear any scratching."

"Why, you have mice," said the crafty old lady. "They will get into your bread and cheese and foul all your food."

There were no mice, but the old woman had implanted mice into the brain of the bride and soon she thought she heard scratching. The following day the old woman arrived with a black-and-white cat. "This is my own sweet Grimalkin," she said, "he thrives on killing mice, the darling. He will rid your house and in a few days I will come to take him home."

About an hour later the cat had vanished, and Letty assumed that he had found his way home. Grimalkin did return home and the old woman hid him in a neighbor's barn. Several days later she returned to the bride and asked for the cat. "He disappeared the day he came," said the young woman, "and I was sure he had run home."

"I haven't seen hide nor hair of him!" Granny Greedle screamed. "My house is plagued with mice, a dozen at once ran off with half a Cheshire cheese." Tears ran down her wrinkles. "I have reared him from a kitten and there has never been such a nonesuch for killing mice. Once he caught two at once, one with his left paw, one with his right."

The old woman added that a cat spotted like that was a rarity in the village and gave rise to the old saying:

A coal-black cat with snowy loins,
Is worth its weight in silver coins.

Then Granny Greedle stomped out, assuring the lass that by this measure Grimalkin was worth fifteen pounds of silver coins.

Letty was astounded at the value put on the cat. She consulted her father-

in-law, who was aware of the old woman's larcenous character. "Did she ever borrow anything from you?" Letty asked.

"Oh, once long ago she borrowed an old wooden ladle not worth one farthing," he told her. "That was all ever." But Letty ran off, satisfied.

A feline felony

When Granny Greedle turned up the next day to collect the silver, the bride asked for the ladle. The old lady expressed surprise and said that children had been playing with the ladle in the dirt and that it had been used for kindling.

"Since you want value for the cat and I want value for the ladle, there is nothing for it but to go before a magistrate," Letty said.

Granny Greedle chuckled to herself at the stupidity of country girls. Since it was clear that a cat was worth more than a wooden ladle, she was certain to win the case and add the silver coins to the stash under her feather bed.

In the courtroom the young woman courteously let the old woman go first. Granny Greedle sang the virtues of Grimalkin, the marvel of catdom. She raved, she ranted, never in the history of the world had there ever been such a peerless feline. The cat, she assured the judge, was worth a thousand ladles and all she was asking for was a mere fifteen pounds of silver.

Rustics sometimes learn shrewdness from the proximity of foxes. Letty claimed that the value of the cat was way offset by the value of the ladle.

In the moon overhead, at its full,
*   you can see*
The trunk, branch and leaf of a
*   cinnamon tree.*

One windy night a branch from such a tree had been blown down in front of her father-in-law's cottage and he had whittled a ladle from the moon-struck wood. Whatever the ladle was dipped into – soup, beer, money – never decreased. The contents remained the same despite the amount on the ladle, Letty assured the judge. And the old woman had thrown that wondrous ladle into the fire!

The judge, on hearing this absurd tale, understood that the marvels of the cat had been a pretext for extortion. He ruled that the two claims canceled each other out. Granny Greedle glared at Letty and stalked off, outsmarted by a country girl and deprived of gainful unemployment.

– Adapted from an English folk tale

111

Edgar Cayce

Modern Nostradamus

EDGAR Cayce, the "Sleeping Prophet," would lie down on his couch and fall into a trance. Hands folded over stomach, Cayce accessed a realm of time and space that allowed him to answer an astounding variety of questions. Some were simple: "How does one remove a wart?" Other answers dealt with profound matters revealing secrets of the universe. Whatever the question, the process remained the same. Cayce would give a "reading" in the self-induced sleep state. A stenographer would ask him questions and write the answers. A copy of the reading went to the originator of the question and a copy went into Cayce's records. Many of the documents from his forty-three years of readings still exist in the archives of the Association for Research and Enlightenment, Inc., in Virginia Beach, Virginia.

Cayce answered thousands of medical questions. In most cases he emphasized the importance of diet, attitudes, emotions, exercise, and the patient's role in the treatment of illness – in effect, Cayce is considered the father of holistic medicine. He communicated specifics about how diet affects our overall health, although he didn't follow his own advice.

Cayce's recommendations from readings included avoiding red meat, white bread, fried foods, and a preference for fruits and leafy vegetables rather than starches. His readings also advised abstaining from alcohol, except for red wine. Cayce advocated both coffee and pure tobacco cigarettes, claiming them harmless. He also suggested that some combinations of foods in the daily diet could be unwholesome: coffee with milk or sugar, citrus with starchy foods, and high- protein fare with starches. If this sounds familiar, they reflect suggestions that have recently turned up in popular diets.

Hits and errors

The readings were not limited to matters of health; Cayce was virtually a modern-day Nostradamus. Although most of his predictions have not come true, Cayce stressed repeatedly that free will influenced all facets of what would become reality. He erred in predicting the rise of Atlantis in the late sixties and also that California would sink into the Pacific. But he correctly foretold the beginning and end of World War I and World War II and the end of the Depression. Cayce first warned of racial strife in the United

States in the 1920s, and in 1939 he predicted the deaths of two presidents in office. Cayce presaged a shift in the earth's axis by the year 2001 that would bring on reversals in climate. Many of today's scientists believe that, along with global warming, a shift in the earth's axis is occurring consistent with results suggested by the Sleeping Prophet. The date is a few years off, but the prediction seems valid in terms of available data.

Interestingly, Cayce's view on astrology stemmed from his view of reincarnation. He claimed that it wasn't necessarily the planets that influenced our souls at the time of birth. Rather he believed that we choose the time of our birth to coincide with the planetary energies. According to Cayce, we carry our abilities and talents from one life-time to another, and the life we lead in the present results from the influences of our former lives. Cayce also spoke about "planetary sojourns," which occur in the time between incarnations. Here we experience the influences of the planets, felt by us in the form of "inclinations, tendencies and urges" that we bring forward into our next lifetime.

Cayce's work has engendered much criticism. Some detractors have called him a false prophet, offering only commonsense and family medicine in answer to questions. Nonetheless many people refer to his health readings for answers to their medical problems today, fifty years after his death. Beyond the medical material, archives of Cayce's work offer a treasure of fascinating reading.

– LENURA BARD

*Fanciful picture of a medieval astronomer trying to discover
the secrets behind the Milky Way, from an Old German engraving*

The Pendulum
Tuning in to hidden tidings

ONE DAY a terrible smell drifted up from the cellar. Two men answering my distress call came and took a look. Did I know where the sewer line was? It was an old house. No one alive knew where those pipes were buried. One of the city workers spun around and headed for the truck. Before I could say, "Hey, wait!" he returned with a set of dowsing rods. As he marched across the lawn it was a matter of seconds before the rods crossed and he pronounced, "It's here." He was right.

Since then I've learned that dowsing is used worldwide in drilling, mining, locating missing persons, diagnosing faulty equipment and discovering archaeological sites. Corporations include it in their budget. Professionals support themselves on dowsing services alone. It's been around for over nine thousand years and simply put, it works.

Dowsing is also known as radiesthesia or detecting information at a distance. It has been practiced in one way or another all over the world. Older accounts surround it with superstition. In Sweden, for instance, the instructions to make a magical dowsing rod were to first find a mountain ash tree grown from a seed that was dropped from a bird's beak. A wand from its branch could then be cut three days after Lady's Day and must never be allowed to touch the ground, steel or iron.

Fortunately a pendulum doesn't require us to jump through nearly so many hoops. As the most popular dowsing tool, it fits in a pocket or can be made on the spot, providing experienced users with fine degrees of response.

Evidence of pendulums exist as early as the seventeenth century. A Saxony museum collection circa 1664 to 1749 contains a pendulum used by the miners' guild. In 1799 Professor Gerboin published research he did with a pendulum he obtained in India.

The French Abbot Mermet is known as the Father of Radiesthesia. Once he was engaged to find water for a village in the Alps. After several attempts, he reported he would have more luck finding gold than water. When asked to prove it, his pendulum led him to a man working in a field, who promptly denied he possessed any gold. Mermet narrowed the search down to the worker's belt and after a moment the field hand recalled that his mother had sewn some gold coins into the back of his belt when he was young.

More recently, the U.S. Navy found out the hard way how well pendulums work when Verne Cameron mapdowsed the location of both U. S. and Soviet submarines in the Pacific.

Good vibes?

No one truly knows how a pendulum works. Through it, libraries of information otherwise deemed unavailable can be accessed through the operator's nervous system. Perhaps the diviner is accessing the superconscious that connects all humans about which Jung theorized. That the world is composed of vibrations has certainly been established. Everything is in constant motion, whether we can see it or not. Each object has an electromagnetic field, humming to its own unique frequency. Could it be that the pendulum is tuning in to these vibrations, and by synchronizing itself with the object, person or place in question, accessing the answers we seek?

To this day, Polish girls string a ring through a lock of their hair and hold it over a glass of water on St. Edward's Day. By counting the rotations, the age they will marry will be revealed. Then, holding the pendulum over her hand, a young woman can count the number of times the pendulum stops between rotations to reveal how many children she will have – clockwise for boys and counterclockwise for girls. One woman recalls counting the rotations as a young girl and could not believe that she would be so old when she married. But the pendulum spoke truly – she was thirty-two years old on her wedding day.

Like any other form of divination, the pendulum requires regular and disciplined use to achieve reliable answers. T. C. Lethbridge believed only two-thirds of the population could master it. Most believe, however, that anyone can learn to use a pendulum with disciplined, regular study. As with all things, the more energy and time devoted to it, the more reliable it will become.

Making a pendulum

Prior experience with meditation is extremely helpful in learning to dowse. Entering a light meditative trance before using the pendulum offers several advantages. It increases focus and helps separate emotions and distractions from the divining process.

Which pendulum you use is a matter of preference. Some become attached to very specific designs, while others are comfortable assembling a pendulum on the spot when the need arises. Both are equally effective. All the pendulum's parts should be composed of non-conductive materials. Black is the most receptive color, should that be an option. Some pendulum bobs open to reveal a cavity that can hold samples, such as gold or a hair, to bring the pendulum into closer sympathy with the person, place or thing being divined.

You can make a pendulum by hanging a symmetrical object, a button or ring, for instance, from a hair or thread no longer than 12 inches. The string is then held between your thumb and forefinger in a free-swinging position. Some diviners prefer to wrap the thread around the tip of a rod, slowly unwinding it in the process of establishing the length at which the pendulum performs best.

Your choice of a pendulum also depends on its intended use. For finer workings, like medical or map dowsing, a lighter bob weighing no more than half an ounce is sufficient. If, however, you intend to walk with your pendulum or use it outside – for water dowsing or finding lost objects – you would be better off with a heavier bob of up to five ounces. The weight will counteract any effects of the wind or body movement. While some people prefer wood, agate or brass pendulums and others prefer materials associated with the operator's sun sign, others have no particular preference.

Yes, no, maybe

The first thing to do when you pick up a pendulum is to program in the movements desired for the answers "yes," "no" and "maybe." One method indicates a "yes" when the pendulum swings in a clockwise motion, "no" with a counterclockwise motion, and "maybe" with a back-and-forth swing in the two o'clock position. Finally, if the answer is not available, the pendulum is programmed to remain still or vibrate erratically in the center.

To program your pendulum, hold the string steadily between the thumb and forefinger of your dominant hand. It is important you do not attempt to make the pendulum move. The pendulum can even be successfully used by people with tremors as long as they are not attempting to influence the direction in which the pendulum swings.

Begin by shortening the string to between one and two inches. The rule is the heavier the bob, the longer the string needed to operate it. Slowly lengthen the string until it begins to swing in a smooth clockwise motion. If your string length is correct, you should be able to operate it blindfolded. If it has a small rotation at first, ask for a larger circle and check whether the movement is improved by lengthening the string. Speak to the pendulum as you would another person, telling it, "This is a yes." Tell the pendulum to be still and then direct it to move counterclockwise and say, "This is a no." The pendulum may not respond to you initially. If you devote a short time each day to practicing, within a few days it will react. After a week of practice, the pendulum should be answering to your verbal instructions.

You will then be ready to ask questions. Our own psychological intrusions are the largest roadblock to accurate divination. The obvious mistake would be trying to sway the pendulum's reply, but assumptions and prejudices, conscious or unconscious, could affect the reading as well. And if you have difficulty focusing, the pendulum could end up responding to a random thought.

Great thinkers of the world, including Albert Einstein, Sir Isaac Newton, Thomas Edison and Leonardo da Vinci, used dowsing to unveil information that would have been unavailable by other means. Wouldn't you, too, like an entire world of information at your fingertips before making an important decision?

– NIALLA NI MACHA

For further details about the pendulum visit www.TheWitchesAlmanac.com/almanacextras2008.

Mount Meru

Jeweled Heart of the Universe

MOUNT MERU, mythological residence of gods, is a legend that resonates in many faiths. The site is considered by believers to be an axis on which the universe itself turns. Buddhists, Hindus, Bonpo and Jains consider its traditions sacred. The myth has a geographical association with Mount Kailash, a four-sided formation with a deep ravine along one face. The elevation rises more than 22,000 feet above the desolate Tibetan Plateau in the Himalayan range. Mount Kailash lies close to the center of the earth's belly at 90 degrees latitude. The site is the source of four of the longest rivers in Asia – the Indus, Ganges, Sutlej and Brahmaputra. The journey to this remote mountain, its circumambulation and mystical associations are considered to confer great spiritual merit.

However mythological, descriptions of Mount Meru are firmly established. With its pyramidlike structure, the mountain is depicted as a great jewel or crystal in Hindu and Tibetan legends. The faces correspond to four directions, each of which is overseen by a guardian spirit, similar to the Western magical concept of elemental watchtowers. In the Hindu texts, the *Puranas*, these faces are described as being made of crystal, ruby, gold and lapis lazuli. The mountain's location lies near the entrance to Shambala, a magical kingdom found only by those with spiritual sight.

In both Hindu and Buddhist myths, Mount Meru has its roots in hell and its peak in heaven. This elaborate system of hells and heavens is often depicted as a mandala in religious art. The four faces also signify the four races of humanity, four primeval continents and the four great rivers that water them. Comparison of these myths with the world known to the ancient peoples of this region is what anchors the mythic mountain to Mount Kailash, although there are some theories that place Mount Meru at the South Pole. For centuries, however, pilgrims have "voted with their feet." For them, the legend and the place are one at Mount Kailash, the name of which means "crystal" in Sanskrit. Its location in the midst of six mountain ranges is likened to the center of a lotus with the surrounding mountains making up the petals.

Hindu legends

The structure of Hindu temples and *stupas*, the shrines, are shaped to represent this holy mountain. And the Hindu *Shri yantra*, the geometric symbol with its interlocking triangles, becomes Mount Meru when viewed in three dimensions. The name "Shri" is synonymous with Lakshmi, the Hindu goddess of wealth and fertility, while Lord Shiva, the supreme yogi, god of destruction and regeneration, is believed to reside on Mount Meru. The interlocking triangles of the *yantra* symbolize, among other things, the dance of Shiva and Shakti – masculine and feminine, ascending and descending power, fire and water, energy and matter – in the creation, destruction and renewal of our world. The sacred sound *aum* is said to be the sound made by the *axis mundi* as it turns.

According to Mount Meru mythology, Indra (some say Brahma), the creator, resides in a golden palace at the summit, along with all the divinities of the Hindu pantheon. It is Shiva and his consort Parvati who reside at Mount Kailash as well as in mythical Meru. Shiva's fierce yogic meditation is said to maintain our world, keeping demonic spirits at bay. Hindu pilgrims make this journey to honor him. Lake Mansowar, at the base of Mt. Kailash is said to represent Parvati, Shiva's consort and divinity of femininity. The lake forms the yoni to the lingam of the mountain, representing the unity of these gender powers in creation. One of the spirits tamed by Shiva, Naga, a great serpent, lives beneath the mountain. His release will symbolize the end of our present age. For Hindu pilgrims, to complete the journey around the base of the mountain is to attain freedom from the delusions of our material world and become more like Shiva, the supreme yogi.

Buddhist beliefs

Tibetan Buddhist iconography of Mount Meru, or Mount Sumeru, as they call it, is complex. The mountain is visualized in the center of a great plain, surrounded by oceans containing the four primeval continents, home of the world's four peoples. The edge of this oceanic plain is ringed with mountains, circled in space by the sun and the 28 mansions of the moon. Above the holy mountain lie multiple heaven realms and below, numerous hells. Similar to the Hindu beliefs, Mount Sumeru is the point at which all the known worlds meet and spin in their orbits. From this movement, the essential sound *aum* emits ceaselessly, permeating all worlds with its vibration.

Buddhist pilgrims believe the holy mountain is the abode of the cosmic Buddha forms of Chakrasamvra and Vajrayogini. While they have individual aspects and are depicted separately, here at Mount Sumeru, as with Shiva and Parvati, they are shown in sexual union and are considered one being. This depiction symbolizes the union of skillful means and wisdom to produce the "bliss of emptiness" known as enlightenment. The name Chakrasamvra means "Wheel of Bliss." This state may also be characterized as the realization of all things without clinging to any one thing. To journey to the mountain and complete a clockwise circuit of its base path is believed to bring the pilgrim closer to this union within one's self. A *mala*, a cycle of 108 circuits, is said to confirm enlightenment.

Bon mythology

Bonpo, practitioners of the shamanic religion of Tibet, call the mountain Tisé. They consider it to be the seat of all spiritual power and its region the holiest place in the world. The mountain is the place that Shenrab, the founder of Bon, is said to have descended from heaven. Like the members of the Jain religion, the Bonpo make the journey around the mountain counterclockwise. Such a journey confers spiritual and metaphysical powers upon the pilgrim. The mountain is also the historic site of a magical duel between the great Bonpo shaman Naro-Bonchung and the Buddhist adept Milarepa over which religion would predominate in Tibet. Milarepa bested Naro-Bonchung by riding the rays of the sun to the summit of the mountain and Tibetan Buddhism became the new religion of Tibet.

Jain tradition

Jain philosophy stresses nonviolence, ascetic practices and individual responsibility for realizing liberation, or *moksha*. This philosophy inspired Mahatma Gandhi's principles of nonviolent resistance that led to Indian independence. Jains believe that 24 Tirthankars (enlightened human beings) exist in all places and times. The first Tirthankar of our place and time, Lord Rishabha, attained *moksha* at the mountain, which the Jain call Mount Ashtapada. Pilgrims make the journey counterclockwise to honor him and visit the site of his enlightenment.

The pilgrim's way

In all accounts of the holy mountain, only supernatural beings may set foot upon its slopes. For any human, such desecration is believed to bring great ill-fortune and has rarely been attempted. The circumambulation ritual is performed around its base.

Since the Chinese takeover of Tibet, travel routes around Mount Kailash have been restricted. Only a couple of routes are generally used now. But many tour companies specialize in getting to the region, one of the most remote in the world. Visitors are generally advised to take a day at a local inn to acclimatize to the altitude. Many tour operators carry oxygen for those who cannot quickly adapt. The pilgrimage around the mountain is challenging, largely due to the altitude.

Tradition grants the greatest merit to two groups of pilgrims: those who complete the journey in one day, which takes a healthy acclimated person over 15 straight hours, or those who complete the journey by doing traditional prostrations the entire way, which takes at least four days. During this circumference, the clear air and breathtaking scenery do much to open a devotee's mind to the thought of enlightenment. For these hardy ones, this journey is the ultimate pilgrimage. Around the route may be found prayer flags, offerings to the spirits and on many rocks, painstakingly carved, the following salutation: *Aum mani padmi hum. Om*, O jewel lotus one.

To believers, Mount Meru is just that, the jewel at the center of the universe.

– ELIZABETH ROSE

119

Flowers of Dreams

POPPIES HAVE HAD a strange mythology down the ages. Seen waving in the fields, the plants look innocuous enough. They grow from two to three feet tall and gorgeous vivid flowers appear from April to August. They last only a few days, and when the petals flutter to the ground bulging seed capsules appear. The tiny seeds, gray or brown, yield fine oil. The leaves, stems and capsules contain a milky juice which turns brown when dried; raw opium. The opium may be processed into the related narcotics that wreak havoc in the lives of addicts, but for ages played a role in ceremony and ritual.

Often the myths encompassed sleep, dreams or death. Poppies were considered sacred to Hypnos, the god of sleep in ancient Greece. Pictures and friezes depicted Hypnos with poppy heads in his hands and adorning his head. Poppies surrounded the doorway to his realm. Hypnos brought prophetic dreams and soothed the pain of those suffering from emotional agony. Romans called this god Somnus, derived from the plant's Latin name, *Papaver somniferum* "bringer of sleep."

In a more sinister guise, the poppy has an Underworld connection and links with Thanatos or Hades, Greek lords of death. Archaeological finds at certain ancient burial sites confirm the poppy's status as a sacred plant intimately connected with the rites of passage to the Underworld. Hades was said to have worn a cap that rendered him invisible when he abducted Persephone. Some mythologists believe that his cap was an allusion to this fantastic flower. An ancient recipe for invisibility advised steeping poppy seeds in wine for fifteen days, then drinking a glass of the brew for five consecutive days while fasting. The potion was then believed to make a person invisible at will.

Poppies were sacred to Demeter, the earth goddess who taught mankind the art of wheat and barley cultivation. During the long search for her abducted daughter Persephone, Demeter was said to have found some

120

relief from her pain by taking opium. Poppies are companion plants of wheat and barley, and the round-bellied, seed-filled capsules were regarded as a symbol of fertility. Poppies also played an important role in Demeter's sacred rites at Eleusis.

Myths assure us that poppies sprang from the tears of Aphrodite when she mourned for Adonis. Cyprus, the birthplace of the love goddess, actively cultivated poppies and from this region opium first made its way to Egypt. The Egyptians valued the narcotic for its allegedly aphrodisiac properties, puzzling in view of its stupefying nature. Legend has it that Cleopatra mixed an opiate in a potion of palm wine and a variety of nightshade. Apparently its intent was not lethal, for it was used as a sedative, painkiller, to calm hysterics, to relieve melancholy, and heal colic, diarrhea and coughs. Egyptians also used opium to heal wounds, abscesses and oddly enough on its medicinal menu, scalp complaints.

An elixir similar to Cleopatra's version turned up in seventeenth-century England. Dr. Thomas Sydenham developed laudanum, containing opium, saffron, cinnamon and cloves, all macerated in wine. Laudanum turned up in patent medicines of the time with no legal restrictions. The concoction made its way to the New World a century later, and during the Civil War its medicinal use on battlefields soared. Its addictive properties unrecognized, some of the first serious cases of opium addiction in the West developed with the excessive wartime use of laudanum.

Opium poppies have never been grown here and in fact their cultivation is illegal. But an indigenous and less potent variety has a history among Native American tribes in the Southwest and in regions of Central America. This species, the prickly poppy, *Argemone mexicana*, is a spiky version of its more powerful cousin. The Aztecs, like the ancient Greeks, also used opiates for healing and ceremonial purposes – and identified the plant with the Underworld. For people who have suffered addiction, the ancient association with the abyss may be readily perceived.

– ARWYNN

Reviews

WALT DISNEY: The Triumph of the American Imagination by Neal Gabler. Illus. 851 pp. Knopf, $35

WHEN WALT Disney's image arises a superb mythologist doesn't tend to be our first association, but the term is fair enough. The creative genius that is Disney took much of his inspiration from the raw material of folk and fairy tales. He put the time-tested stories through his mental cooker, dished them up in animation, and served them forth in a new stew of antic delights. The flavoring was Disney's own dimension of fantasy that trumped reality, enchanting America and ultimately the world.

From the earliest efforts of the 1920s Disney produced "Puss in Boots," "The Four Musicians of Bremen," "Goldilocks and the Three Bears," and "Little Red Riding Hood." He offered more of the same through the following decade, including "Playful Pan," "Hell's Bells," "Mother Goose Melodies," and my own personal favorite by name, "Cannibal Capers."

Yoo hoo, Mickey! Here we go, from mythologist to wizard, for the great American icon issued from Disney's own teeming brain and derived from we can't imagine what. The squeaky sweetie made his debut in 1928 as "Steamboat Willie." Minnie was also aboard, although Mickey was the star from the first outing. Minnie's dialogue mainly consisted of "Oh, Mickey!" Minnie couldn't keep up with Mickey. Pluto, that hapless human in a doggie suit, also turned up from the start.

We meet the whole cast of characters as Disney created them in Neal Gabler's comprehensive biography, seven years in the creation. Gabler brings the artist into sharp focus. It is a daunting 851-page doorstop of a book, although 218 pages are lists of resources, an adventure in anal retention.

The studio became a factory of cartooniana during the twenties and thirties. But as popular worldwide as the films were, Disney always tottered on the edge of ruin, falling from an economic cliff like a cartoon character in peril frantically pedaling his way through midair. But as the thirties wound down, the popularity of this mighty mouse was overtaken by a firequacker of a duck. People loved the spin-off's attitude – Donald always seemed mad as hell, wasn't going to take it any more, and his frenzied quacking had audiences in hysterics.

In 1937 Disney presented his masterpiece, the stunning "Snow White and the Seven Dwarfs," based on a story by the Grimms. Four years in the making, it was the first feature-length animation, before its release known around Hollywood as "Disney's folly." But Snow White brought Disney his first economic bonanza, grossing a record $6.7 million. The film was followed by "Pinocchio," the "little woodenhead," another masterpiece. To Disney's disappointment, this feature sank both critically and at the box office.

Walt decided that his true love, eclipsed by quackery, should have a "comeback." And so "Fantasia" was planned around Mickey, but the feature resulted in a muddle of mixed media. Some sequences are exquisite, others tedious. But "The Sorcerer's Apprentice" segment, with music by Paul Dukas, is a comedic gem. Mickey attempts to enchant a broom for doing his chores, but he is not up to the magic. The broom runs wild and the untrained apprentice's desperation runs equally wild. But "Fantasia" also tanked. Debt was ever nipping at Walt's heels, and his appetite for work waned. "We're making corn," he told a studio artist, "but it's got to be good corn." Many were not even "good corn" – "Son of Flubber," for instance, and numerous others were equally mawkish.

In 1955 Walt fathered another animal, the cash cow of the first Magical Kingdom. Disneylands and merchandising spins soared to commercial success undreamed of by the artist. A lifelong smoker, Disney died at age sixty-five of lung cancer, but his creations eerily ever increase. The theme parks dot the globe, and yet another Main Street may turn up in Thailand. I have just read elsewhere that the Disney Corporation is checking out webisodes. Maybe Mickey will pop up next in a three-minute ha-ha on your digital phone. Stay tuned!

Songs of Witchcraft & Magic from the British Folk Tradition. Compiled by the Museum of Witchcraft, Boscastle, Cornwall, UK.

FOR THOSE already familiar with the traditional British folk-music style, this delightful collection will be a welcome addition. For those who have yet to discover the charm these tunes carry, a pleasant surprise awaits you. This CD is a must-have for everyone with an interest in British traditional witchcraft. Magic and mystery abound in our cultural history, and it is no coincidence that such matters reflect in our musical heritage as well. This collection brings together the finest artists of the genre and the most haunting ballads to enchant its audience. Treat yourself to a musical journey to the boundary between our present world and the time beyond time. Be ye transformed by these powerful songs and fantastic tales.

Fifteen timeless songs accompanied by 36 pages of lyrics and extensive research into the stories and their meanings. Wild Goose records WGS 341CD.

You may order the CD through The Museum of Witchcraft:
http://www.museumofwitchcraft.com/
Telephone: 01840 250111 (within UK)
Telephone: +44 1840 250111 (intl)
Email: museumwitchcraft@AOL.com

From a Witch's Mailbox

Stirring up, settling down

After picking up the 07-08 Witches' Almanac I was initially pleased with the new glossy cover, but a little unnerved. The binding is beautiful. I have been collecting the Almanacs since the mid-nineties, and my Celtic grandmother before that. It used to be you could only find the Almanac in off-beat locations and now they are found in your local Borders. I can appreciate a business wanting to grow, but I just needed to put my two cents in and to share how much I hope the Almanac will not become something frivolous.

– Amanda
e-mail

Our older readership is very happy to have a larger format with larger print, and our younger readership likes the four-color cover that resists stains and wear and tear. But our distributor had suggested updating the appearance to address the competition. We now have a new cover with an older, more woodcut-type look to it, another turn-around. From time to time things need a little stirring, and after things settle the soup tastes better. The Almanac will stay the current 6x9 size to provide the larger type everyone likes. As for Borders, we have sold to bookstores large and small for many years. Not to worry. The Almanac is the oldest and most respected authority in matters of the occult – and now, as ever, dedicated to excellence.

Pain begone

Do you know of any charm to rid oneself of unrequited love? This is like an affliction, incredibly painful, and seems to go on and on.

– Timothy Ross
Troy, New York

Here is an old charm our late editor, Elizabeth Pepper, once provided. We hope this will help and permit you to move on to a happier love experience.

Kneel before a roaring fire. As you hold a handful of vervain leaves, concentrate upon your intention. Throw the herb all at once on the blaze and repeat:

> *Here is my pain,*
> *Take it up and soar,*
> *Depart from me now,*
> *Offend me no more.*

Beware!

I have heard that birds flying away from the sea presage a storm. Have you ever heard of any other unusual warnings from nature?

– E.C.Y.
Reno, Nevada

That makes sense, and yes, we have heard of other lesser-known storm indicators. (Of course, Chicken Little springs to mind.) It is said that bees won't venture from hives, wolves howl and mice skip around. But we hope you will be spared the wolves and mice.

Poet of the gods

Through the years your articles have repeatedly cited quotations from Hesiod. I have never seen his name elsewhere. Who was he and why is he so often in your pages?

– Elfriede
Palo Alto, California

Hesiod was a Greek poet who lived around 700 B.C., important as a major source of the cosmology based on the oral tradition. Because there was ritual but no orthodoxy, great confusion existed around the identity of the gods. The Greeks turned to two monumental poets to provide spiritual unity and establish order in the cosmos. The works of Homer allowed a more orderly universe to emerge. But according to the latest Almanac publication, Greek Gods in Love, *"The uncluttering was reinforced by Hesiod's Theogony, in which the Muses gave him a poet's voice and bade him 'sing of the race of the blessed gods immortal.' " When we look backward in time and want information about "the blessed gods immortal," we turn to Hesiod.*

Night of the Watchers

I have read every edition of the Almanac since 1972. Each year I have seen the Night of the Watchers entry, June 5, on the Moon Calendar. I am somewhat familiar with the Watchers, but I have long wondered if there was any specific lore attached to that particular night. Could you provide additional insight on this matter? I think that this subject would provide an interesting short article on the lore of the Watchers in a future edition.

– Beverly Brigantia
e-mail

We have taken your advice and the suggestions of other readers and included a Night Watchers article in this issue. You will also find additional information on our website.

Black Fido

When we English are depressed, we are said to have "the black dog." As a dog lover, I would like to know if you are aware of any "good black dog" stories?

– Edwin Palfrey
Bath, England

Sure. We love it when we know the answers to weird questions. British folklore offers a few such stories. We like the one about Johnnie Greenwood, in an emergency needing to cross a dense, frightening forest late at night. He was met by a big black dog that pattered at his side through the woods and then vanished. Returning, Johnnie had the same canine escort. From an account in a local paper, "Years after, two prisoners in York Jail told the chaplain that they had intended to rob and murder Johnnie that night in the wood, but that he had a large dog

with him, and when they saw that, they felt that Johnnie and the dog together would be too much for them."

Now, that's a pretty good black dog.

The never-ending circle

What is the Hecate Wheel?
— Raul Martino
Chicago, Illinois

The Hecate Wheel is an ancient symbol that signifies the eternal nature of witchcraft, and it is used to invoke the Dark Goddess. Its threefold pattern in a never-ending circle is used for contemplation and meditation in Western mysticism.

Waxing, waning

I was glancing at the last issue in Barnes & Noble for Spring 2007-2008 and I noticed you do not have when the moon is waxing and waning printed on your calendar like in the past. Is there some new way you have this in your new almanac or has it been omitted?
— Arlene
Hartford, Connecticut

We eliminated these for space consideration. But other readers also miss the waxing-waning information and we have restored it as part of the feature. Your letter also made us remember a nice little poem from Christina Rossetti that helps us distinguish the phases:

O Lady Moon, your horns
point to the East
Shine, be increased!
O Lady Moon, your horns
point to the West
Wane, be at rest!

Scent of love

Why is jasmine used in so many love charms?
— B.T.
e-mail

The lovely trumpet-shaped flower has long been associated with love because of its hauntingly beautiful scent – and perhaps also because it blooms at night, often the time passion arises.

Let us hear from you, too

We love to hear from our readers. Letters should be sent with the writer's name (or just first name or initials), address, daytime phone number and e-mail address. Published material may be edited for clarity or length. All letters become the property of The Witches' Almanac Ltd. and will not be returned. We regret that owing to the volume of correspondence we cannot reply to every letter.

The Witches' Almanac, Ltd.
P.O. Box 2292
Newport, RI 02840-9998
witchesal@yahoo.com
www.TheWitchesAlmanac.com

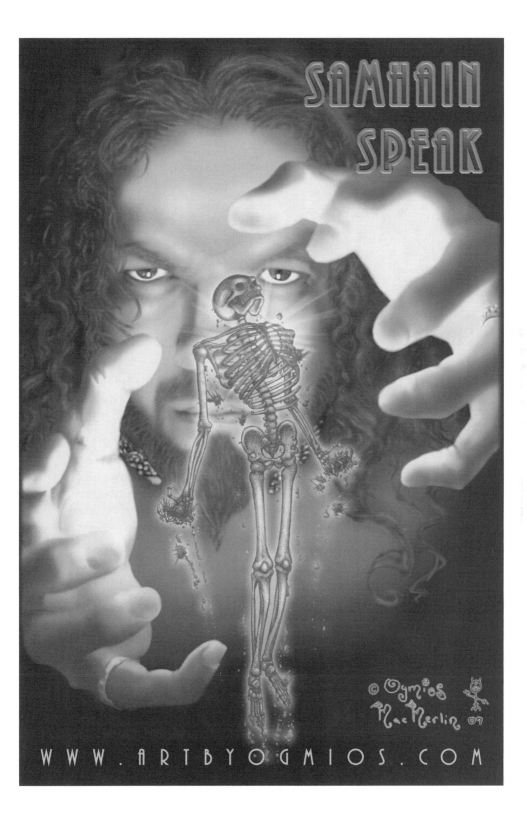

For information, email advertising@TheWitchesAlmanac.com.

❧ CLASSIFIEDS ❧

The Koo Hollie Series of Metaphysical Books
by Dikki-Jo Mullen

WELCOME TO FLORIDA'S *Star of the Sorceress School of Metaphysics.*

Practical instruction in astrology, tarot, yoga, ritual magic, ghost tracking, sacred sites, past life regression and much more is offered in these signed and numbered first edition allegorical novels about a Florida astrologer, Koo Hollie. Over sized spiral bound, illustrated with vintage photos and original calligraphy drawings. The series is adapted from the case books of *The Witches' Almanac* Astrologer and Parapsychologist Dikki-Jo Mullen's professional practice.

Koo Hollie and the Corn Goddess Chronicle

Koo's purchase of the life sized statue of a mysterious century old Native American Princess is the catalyst for this intriguing drama. The adventure moves from an ancient beach house on Florida's Space Coast to a cottage in Orlando to the forgotten village of Uponthee in the Everglades. Crime, murder and government corruption develop as the plot unfolds. $22.00 (please add $4.95 for shipping and handling)

Koo Hollie and the Spirit of Prism Rosa

Prism Rosa was a beautiful and eccentric young woman who wandered the beaches and streets of Florida's oldest city, St. Augustine, during the roaring 20's. Rose's nick-name honored her habit of leaving colored crystal prisms as gifts in unexpected places with little explanation. Nearly a century after Rose's death Koo Hollie finds one of the crystal prisms left hidden in a very haunted Bed and Breakfast. Across time and space Prism Rosa influences the re-opening of the case file on a crime long considered cold. $22.00 (please add $4.95 for shipping and handling)

Koo Hollie and The Eight Phases of the Blue Moon

This allegorical novel is latest in author Dikki-Jo Mullen's popular series. Learn about the stars, protective egg magic, lost continents, crop circles, the eight phases of the Moon, zodiac signs, past life regression, and much more. From the Caribbean islands amid the ruins of Atlantis to the mysterious Native American village of Uponthee in the Florida Everglades to the remote mountains of the Basque region in Europe, the action unfolds beneath an unusual and powerful Blood Blue Moon. $22.00 (please add $4.95 for shipping and handling)

Convention Programs, Personal Readings, Group Presentations available.
PO Box 533024
Orlando, Florida 32853
Phone 407-895-1522 or
321-773-1414

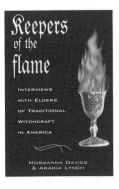

Our books available by mail order:

ℐ Treasury from past editions...

Perfect for study or casual reading, Witches All *is a collection from* The Witches' Almanac *publications of the past. Arranged by topics, the book, like the popular almanacs, is thought provoking and often spurs me on to a tangent leading to even greater discovery.*

The information and art in the book—astrological attributes, spells, recipes, history, facts & figures is a great reminder of the history of the Craft, not just in recent years, but in the early days of the Witchcraft Revival in this century: the witch in a historical and cultural perspective.

Ty Bevington, Circle of the Wicker Man,
Columbus, Ohio

Absolutely beautiful! I recently ordered Witches All *and I have to say I wasn't disappointed. The artwork and articles are first rate and for a longtime* Witches' Almanac *fan, it is a wonderful addition to my collection.* Witches' Almanac *devotees and newbies alike will love this latest effort. Very worth getting.*

Tarot3, Willits, California

MAGIC CHARMS FROM A TO Z

A treasury of amulets, talismans, fetishes and other lucky objects compiled by the staff of *The Witches' Almanac.* An invaluable guide for all who respond to the call of mystery and enchantment.

LOVE CHARMS

Love has many forms, many aspects. Ceremonies performed in witch-craft celebrate the joy and the blessings of love. Here is a collection of love charms to use now and ever after.

MAGICAL CREATURES

Mystic tradition grants pride of place to many members of the animal kingdom. Some share our life. Others live wild and free. Still others never lived at all, springing instead from the remarkable power of human imagination.

ANCIENT ROMAN HOLIDAYS

The glory that was Rome awaits you in Barbara Stacy's classic presentation of a festive year in pagan times. Here are the gods and goddesses as the Romans conceived them, accompanied by the annual rites performed in their worship. Scholarly, light-hearted — a rare combination.

CELTIC TREE MAGIC

Robert Graves in *The White Goddess* writes of the significance of trees in the old Celtic lore. *Celtic Tree Magic* is an investigation of the sacred trees in the remarkable Beth-Luis-Nion alphabet; their role in folklore, poetry, and mysticism.

MOON LORE

As both the largest and the brightest object in the night sky, and the only one to appear in phases, the Moon has been a rich source of myth for as long as there have been mythmakers.

MAGIC SPELLS AND INCANTATIONS

Words have magic power. Their sound, spoken or sung, has ever been a part of mystic ritual. From ancient Egypt to the present, those who practice the art of enchantment have drawn inspiration from a treasury of thoughts and themes passed down through the ages.

LOVE FEASTS

Creating meals to share with the one you love can be a sacred ceremony in itself. With the witch in mind, culinary adept Christine Fox offers magical menus and recipes for every month in the year.

RANDOM RECOLLECTIONS
I, II, III, IV

Pages culled from the original (no longer available) issues of *The Witches' Almanac*, published annually throughout the 1970's, are now available in a series of tasteful booklets. A treasure for those who missed us the first time around; keepsakes for those who remember.

Order form on back page

Good Luck Bracelets

Gemstones are cherished by the wise for their life-enhancing values. The right gems help bring you luck. These matched gems on stretchable one-size-fits-all cords make beautiful accessories. Wear one or more, as long as their purposes do not conflict.

Bracelets are packed in pouches with legends about their properties. Visit our website at www.TheWitchesAlmanac.com to view the bracelets and read their legends. $5.95 each, $2.00 shipping/handling. Wholesale inquiries welcome.

The Witches' Almanac Book Bag

front

back

Tasteful Toting

Complimentary with any purchase over $100, or $17.95 each, $3.00 shipping/handling.

The Witches' Almanac logo and the medieval woodcut design take you through the day in mystic style.

The tasteful canvas bag, measuring 17" x 13" x 5", with a 20" strap, carries whatever you fancy – books, clothes, laptop, cardcase, lunch, water, makeup, secrets, it's your space.

Choice of black on natural or black on red. Wholesale inquiries welcome.

And a special offer – Count on your own free book bag if you order an Almanac Bundle, 13 back issues, $75 (a $117.00 value). 1993/4 through the 2005/6 Almanac.

Greek Gods in Love

Barbara Stacy

*New versions
of timeless love tales —
lively, witty, entertaining*

The author casts a marvelously original eye on the beloved stories of Greek deities, replete with amorous oddities and escapades.

Above them all reigned Zeus. The ancients enjoyed his constant adultery, launched after a 300-year honeymoon with his sister-wife Hera. His affairs were often weird and fanciful, an equal opportunity seducer among goddesses, nymphs and mortals.

If the Glorious One enjoyed such an extravagant sex life, how could poor weak mortals be expected to resist the compelling power of passion?

The glittering mythology resonates with Eros, love in all its astounding variety – devotional, perfidious, sunny, dark, frenzied, serene, lusty, uncanny, earthy, twisty, and sometimes hilarious. We relish these tales in all their splendor and antic humor, and offer an inspired storyteller's fresh version of the old, old mythical magic.

Lavishly illustrated with 190 designs drawn from ancient Greek art. Visual delights abound.

$15.95 Paperback, 120 pages, 9" x 11"

Use the order form on the back page, or order online at *www.TheWitchesAlmanac.com*.

Order Form

Each timeless edition of *The Witches' Almanac* is unique.
Limited numbers of previous years' editions are available.

The Witches' Almanac

___ 2008-2009 @ $10.95 _____
___ 2007-2008 @ $9.95 _____
___ 2006-2007, ___ 2005-2006, ___ 2004-2005, ___ 2003-2004 @ $8.95 _____
___ 2002-2003, ___ 2001-2002, ___ 2000-2001, ___ 1999-2000 @ $7.95 _____
___ 1998-1999, ___ 1997-1998, ___ 1996-1997, ___ 1995-1996 @ $6.95 _____
___ 1994-1995, ___ 1993-1994 @ $5.95 _____
___ Bundle of 13 back issues (*Free book bag*) @ $75.00 _____
___ Witches' All @ $13.95 _____
Random Recollections ___ I, ___ II, ___ III, ___ IV @ $3.95 _____

Bracelets and Book Bags

___ Agate, Green ___ Agate, Moss ___ Agate, Natural ___ Agate, Red @ $5.95 _____
___ Amethyst ___ Aventurine ___ Fluorite ___ Jade, African ___ Jade, White @ $5.95 _____
___ Jasper, Picture ___ Jasper, Red ___ Lapis Lazuli ___ Malachite @ $5.95 _____
___ Moonstone ___ Obsidian ___ Onyx, Black ___ Opal ___ Quartz Crystal @ $5.95 _____
___ Quartz, Rose ___ Rhodonite ___ Sodalite ___ Tigereye @ $5.95 _____
___ Turquoise ___ Unakite @ $5.95 _____
___ Natural/Black Book Bag ___ Red/Black Book Bag @ $17.95 _____

Other Publications

___ Greek Gods In Love @ $15.95 _____
___ Magic Charms from A to Z @ $12.95 _____
___ Love Charms @ $6.95 _____
___ Magical Creatures @ $12.95 _____
___ Ancient Roman Holidays @ $6.95 _____
___ Celtic Tree Magic @ $7.95 _____
___ Moon Lore @ $7.95 _____
___ Magic Spells and Incantations @ $12.95 _____
___ Love Feasts @ $6.95 _____

Send a check or money order
payable in U. S. funds
or credit card details to:
The Witches' Almanac, Ltd.
PO Box 1292
Newport, RI 02840-9998
401)847-3388 (phone)
(888)897-3388 (fax)
Email: info@thewitchesalmanac.com
www.TheWitchesAlmanac.com

Subtotal _____
Shipping & handling _____
(*One book: $4.00 Each additional book add $1.50;*
$2.00 per bracelet; $3.00 per book bag)
Total _____